FROM PALE TO PAMPA

FROM PALE
TO PAMPA

A Social History of
the Jews of Buenos Aires

Eugene F. Sofer

HOLMES & MEIER

New York   London

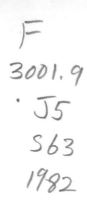

First published in the United States of America 1982 by
Holmes & Meier Publishers, Inc.
30 Irving Place
New York, N.Y. 10003

Great Britain:
Holmes & Meier Publishers, Ltd.
131 Trafalgar Road
Greenwich, London SE10 9TX

Book design by Rose Jacobowitz

Library of Congress Cataloging in Publication Data

Sofer, Eugene F.
  From pale to pampa.

  Bibliography: p.
  Includes index.
    1. Jews—Argentina—Buenos Aires—History. 2. Buenos
Aires (Argentina)—Ethnic relations. I. Title.
F3001.9.J5S63   1981   982'.11   81-6866
ISBN 0-8419-0428-6   AACR2

Manufactured in the United States of America

CONTENTS

ACKNOWLEDGMENTS

I wish to thank the Latin American Center at UCLA, the Institute for Jewish Policy Planning and Research, and the National Foundation for Jewish Culture for their generous financial support while I researched and wrote the dissertation from which this book evolved.

Thanks go to Stephan Thernstrom for his constant support, encouragement, suggestions, and assistance. Mark Szuchman discussed many of the aspects of the dissertation with me in Buenos Aires, Austin, and Los Angeles. Steve Olson edited this manuscript and offered a number of constructive suggestions for its improvement. My thanks, also, to Diane Werner for typing the final manuscript.

Jacobo Kovadloff, former Director of the American Jewish Committee Office in Buenos Aires, and Santiago Kovadloff selflessly offered their assistance and friendship. Dr. Moises Goldman provided crucial support and facilitated my research. Dr. Herman Korin and his family spent hours discussing the history of the community with me and, equally important, made me feel like a member of the family. Osvaldo Natansohn became a close friend, discussed Argentine history with me, and worked tirelessly to make my stays in Buenos Aires enjoyable.

The Associación Mutual Israelita Argentina opened its archives to me, provided me with office space, and extended every conceivable kindness. The staff of Yiddisher Wisnshaftlecher Institut Archives (IWO) Argentina diligently searched out material for me. The Archivo General de la Nación offered every kindness while I worked there.

Robert N. Burr deserves special mention for his support of this project and, more importantly, for all the benefits I derived from our long association. My deepest debt of gratitude is to my wife Judith Bartnoff, who devoted countless hours to the manuscript, kept my spirits up, and helped me to see this project through.

PREFACE

In September 1979, the military government of Argentina, with the full support of Argentina's Supreme Court, expelled Jacobo Timerman, outspoken newspaper publisher and Zionist, from the country. During his three previous years of imprisonment, torture, and house arrest, Timerman had become a worldwide focus for concern over anti-Semitism in Argentina. As the repression that culminated in his exile intensified, there could be no question that one of Timerman's crimes was his Jewishness.

The mistreatment of Timerman and of thousands of other Jews in Argentina has forced the world community, and Jews in particular, to come to grips with the brutality and repression that is Argentina. Newspaper headlines about disappearances and widespread torture have fueled a need for information. What is Argentina like? What is the Jewish community like, and how did it come to be under such virulent attack? How has the community confronted challenges to its existence? Unfortunately, sources of information have always been scarce.

This book focuses on only a few aspects of the rich and complex history of the Jewish community in Argentina. First, it examines only the eastern European Jewish community in Buenos Aires, though this is far and away the most significant Jewish community in the country. Second, it concentrates on establishing links between the occupational and residential mobility of eastern European Jews and the larger patterns of Argentine social and economic history. It also ties these measures of mobility to Argentine politics; this against the constantly fluctuating backdrop of anti-Semitism.

While this study began as an attempt to illuminate certain trends in Argentine history, it cannot help but bear, either directly or indirectly, on the history of Jews throughout the New World. It therefore is important to note that the experiences of Argentine Jews differed in several crucial respects from those of Jews in the United States. I believe that most students of Argentine Jewry have presumed certain universals (implicitly drawn from the history of Jews in New York City) and have, as a result, operated on mistaken assumptions. They often assume that if Jews in New York were upwardly mobile, so must their relatives in Argentina have been. If, after one generation, Jews in New York entered the professions, then Jews must have followed the same pattern in Buenos Aires. To be sure, there were similarities; but there were also important differences. Only by recognizing at the outset that the history of Jews in Argentina is uniquely rooted in the specific conditions of Argentine development can those differences be explored.

Because of the increasingly widespread interest in the history of Argentine Jewry among nonscholars, I have eliminated much of the scholarly apparatus that accompanied the dissertation from which this book has sprung.* Furthermore, the dissertation, completed in 1976, differs from the present work in several additional ways. First, as is the habit with dissertations, it contains a lengthy historiographical essay that underestimates the contributions of others to the field and overestimates my own. It also constructs an argument based on Marc Bloch's work that would facilitate a comparative treatment of the Jewish experience in Buenos Aires, New York, and London. Essentially, the dissertation argues that similarities in the three cases allow extrapolations from two of the cases to the third. Because the historiography of Jews in London and New York is so much richer and more extensive than the historiography of Jews in Argentina, the dissertation used this framework to speculate on what might have taken place in Buenos Aires. There was no need to include either the argument or its conclusion in this book.

The dissertation also included a more full-blown discussion of the quantitative methods I used, a matter of little interest to the general public. To be absolutely explicit, I do not claim that the data I present are statistically significant; they are necessarily too fragmentary and incomplete to meet the statistician's rigors. But I do believe that the data are historically suggestive and that, in conjunction with qualitative evidence, they offer an accurate view of the Jewish community's history in Buenos Aires.

Although the dissertation treated only the period between the first widespread immigration of Jews into Argentina at the end of the nineteenth century and the end of World War II, this book includes a final chapter that brings the history up to date and offers an analytical framework for comprehending the Jewish community's travails in Argentina since 1973.

---

*The dissertation, for those who wish to pursue the topic in more depth and less clarity, is available from University Microfilms.

A final note: the cooperation of the Asociacíon Mutual Israelita Argentina (AMIA), the successor of the Chevrah formed in Buenos Aires in 1895, made possible this research. The only condition imposed upon me was that I not use the names of individuals. I have honored that request by using first names and last initials only. I hope that this solution to a thorny problem both protects and honors those whom I have studied.

CHAPTER 1   **INTRODUCTION**

In 1891, Chaim Kinderman, a tailor who had been expelled from Moscow by the tsar's most recent anti-Semitic decree, told two U. S. investigators visiting Russia that his business had been ruined, that his savings had been wiped out, and that he was now virtually unemployable. With no hope for a better future in Russia, he and the seven members of his family had applied for permission to emigrate to Argentina. Nochin Haiser, once the owner of a factory that manufactured cigarette holders, expressed to the investigators his own desire to go to Argentina. He explained that he already had one daughter in America and that he wanted to take his two sons and join her in a country where a man could make an honest living. Meyer Abrahamson, a 40-year-old watchmaker with two daughters, who had been expelled from Moscow after having lived there legally since 1879, told the Americans that he couldn't go to the Pale of Settlement because of the overabundance of watchmakers there. Abrahamson wanted to emigrate to Argentina, and his daughters, a bit confused about the geography of the New World, were learning English so that they would be prepared for their new home.[1]

For these Jews, and thousands others like them, Argentina embodied new cause for hope. If not the Promised Land, it was at least a land of promise.

From 1889, when the steamship *Weser* carrying 130 Jewish families docked in Buenos Aires, until 1930, when the military government of President José F. Uriburu drastically curtailed immigration to fight unemployment, Argentina attracted more eastern European Jews (Ashkenazim) than any other country except the United States. These Jews, doubtlessly unprepared for their arduous journey, immediately confronted new obstacles and new opportunities. The lands from which they emigrated—Russia, Poland, and Rumania—barely resembled the country to which they came. Some found their new surroundings accommodating; in the words of one, "admirably suited as a new home, being free, tolerant as regards religion, healthy and of fruitful soil." Others were not so enthusiastic, including one immigrant so appalled he concluded that "the recommendation of Russian Jewish emigration [to Argentina] would amount to a crime."[2]

Ill-advised or not, Jews continued to disembark at Buenos Aires to seek out relatives, friends, and neighbors. They found jobs and made homes; they established institutions and organizations. In short, they became an integral part of Argentina's developing society. Their adaptation to their new home is the focus of this study.

In spite of recent scholarly and journalistic assessments of Argentine Jewry, we actually know very little about the community's history. Argentine Jews have written some memoirs and studies of Jews in the colonial period, but most concentrate on the famous "Jewish gauchos," who very early ceased to be representative of the immigrant experience. With few exceptions most others have emphasized the internal history of the community; more recently, anti-Semitism, which comprises only a limited part of their total history, has been the subject of published writings.[3]

The first organized immigrants, numbering more than 800, sought to establish an agricultural colony in Santa Fe Province in 1889. They soon found, however, that desire could not overcome their inexperience or compensate for the harsh realities of life on the pampas. In 1891, the Jewish Colonization Association (JCA), endowed by European railroad magnate and financier Baron Maurice de Hirsch, assumed the burden of their support. Hirsch hoped that "the time will come when I shall have from three to four hundred thousand Jews flourishing on their homesteads in the Argentine, peaceful and respected citizens, a valuable source of national wealth and stability. Then we shall be able to point to them and contrast them with their brethren who have been demoralized by persecution. What will the Jew-haters have to say then?"[4]

Hirsch's representatives in Argentina nourished his utopian hopes. David Feinberg reported to him that

> In the course of my journeys through the colonies, I came across several families whom I had personally known in Russia. I recognized them no longer. It was not the lean and pitiful-looking Jew, with hollow cheeks and bent shoulders, . . . with a visage full of indefinable expression of sadness and constant care; in a word it was no longer the man seeking his daily bread without ever gaining it, whom I saw before me. . . . The free and healthy care of the country, physical labour and etc., have completely transformed them.[5]

Such encounters could not have been common. The colonies

meant locusts, Indians, hostile neighbors, and disease. In the end, the baron's dreams of a Jewish yeomanry foundered on the problems of Argentine rural life. In 1895, only 13.3 percent of Argentina's Jews lived in Buenos Aires; by 1935, only 11 percent lived on the land.

SETTLEMENT IN BUENOS AIRES

The optimistic immigrants of the late nineteenth century turned from rural life to Buenos Aires, which was rapidly modernizing with the profits of Argentina's export economy. Today, 80 percent of the country's Jews and almost half of all Argentines reside in Buenos Aires and its environs, which for over a century has been a powerful magnet to those seeking opportunity. The overwhelming dominance of this port city was a result of Argentina's skewed economic development. From the eighteenth century on, Argentine food exports fueled Europe's Industrial Revolution; in return, European manufactured goods passed through Buenos Aires on their way to the interior. The *entrepôt* monopolized customs revenues. Thus the city and province of Buenos Aires grew wealthier, while the interior provinces grew poorer and even more dependent on the port's niggardly largesse.

Both *provincianos* (residents of the provinces) and *porteños* (residents of the city of Buenos Aires) hoped that the federalization of Buenos Aires in 1880 would solve this lingering and divisive problem. In fact, it only made it worse. Federalization "had as its political objective the subjugation of the porteños and the appropriation of the port's wealth, prestige and power for the national benefit. The result, however, was that the city captured the nation."[6] Legislation could not alter the facts that most of the population and the bulk of agricultural production, manufacturing, and communication centers were concentrated in the relatively limited area surrounding the city of Buenos Aires.

Massive immigration added to an indigenous population boom, and in the two decades after 1895 the number of Argentines doubled to about eight million. Between 1914 and 1947, the population again increased by 100 percent. Though the number of Argentines increased by leaps and bounds, the demographic growth of Buenos Aires outstripped even that of the nation. In 1895, about 19 percent of Argentina's total population lived in Buenos Aires and its environs; in 1947, three out of every ten Argentines lived in metropolitan Buenos Aires.[7] By the outbreak of World War I, seven times as many people lived in Buenos Aires as in Argentina's second largest city.

THE JEWISH MIGRATION

The fluidity of Jewish immigration to Argentina, the reluctance of many Jews to reveal their religious preferences to government authorities, and an illegal flow of unknown dimensions have always prevented an accurate enumeration of how many Jews lived in Argentina at any given time. We do know that during the first decade of mass immigration many Jews left Argentina for the United States, other countries in Latin America, or Russia. As many as 1,000 returned to Russia between 1892 and 1900, for example. But most of those who left went to the United States, almost 2,000 in 1907 alone.[8]

Nevertheless, immigration by eastern European Jews did contribute significantly to Argentina's population growth. In 1895, about 7,500 Jews lived in Argentina, most of them in the colonies. By 1909, however, more than one third of the country's 50,000 Jews resided in Buenos Aires. The attractions of Buenos Aires to immigrants and disgruntled colonists alike continued to dictate population trends in the years to follow. Between 1920 and 1935, because of the Depression and a decrease in agricultural prices, the population of the Jewish colonies declined precipitously. By the late 1940s, the number of colonists fell below the number present in 1896. When the Moisesville colony celebrated its 75th anniversary in 1964, only 1,686 families were still connected to the JCA colonies.

Meanwhile, the Jewish population increased from 120,000 to about 230,000 between 1920 and 1936, more than half of whom lived in Buenos Aires. By 1947, approximately 200,000 Jews, fully 75 percent of Argentine Jewry, lived in metropolitan Buenos Aires, which at that time boasted close to five million people.[9] Jews, at least 85 percent of them of Ashkenazic origins, had come to comprise Argentina's third largest immigrant group.

Whether Argentina was indeed a "melting pot" is of crucial importance to understanding the country's current condition. According to the influential Argentine sociologist Gino Germani, because of immigration "the two-strata system of the mid-nineteenth century was replaced by a much more complex structure," and "social mobility became a normal pattern in Argentine society (or at least in the central areas). . . ." Further, according to Germani, "the immigrants' upward mobility facilitated the acculturation of their children. Often the second generation was assimilated into a different social class, values, style of living and expectations that greatly diverged from those of the previous generation."[10] If Germani is correct, the roots of the prolonged crisis that Jews in Argentina are now undergoing may well lie (as he would contend) in psychocultural, rather than social, factors. If, on the other hand, Argentina offered less to its immigrants than he makes out, it should be possible to arrive at an explanation of the country's failure to fulfill its promise that is more objective than "defects in the character of the Argentine people."[11]

OCCUPATIONAL MOBILITY

The importance of imigration, in which Jews played a major role, to Argentine history cannot be exaggerated. The prevailing interpretation of its impact argues that immigration transformed Argentina from a traditional society to a mass society, one characterized by greater political participation (at least electorally), a less rigid class structure, and a high degree of occupational mobility. Some scholars have recently chipped away at this interpretation by questioning the extent to which immigrants participated in the political process. Few, however, have challenged the interpretation with respect to Argentine social mobility.[12]

In treating the Jewish experience as a case study of Argentine immigration, I have chosen to focus on four themes: community life, political interaction between the community and the state, residential mobility, and occupational mobility. The first two, which I examine qualitatively, are straightforward and self-evident. The latter two, which I treat quantitatively, and particularly the last, require a bit of explanation.

Stephan Thernstrom has noted that "the historical study of social mobility requires the use of objective criteria of social status. The most convenient of these is occupation. Occupation may be only one variable in a comprehensive theory of class, but it is the variable that includes more, that sets more limits on the other variables than any other criterion of status."[13] Once industrialized, the division of labor in relatively complex societies like Argentina is fairly stable, so occupational change over generations, as well as over the working life of an individual, is a convenient way to measure change. Thus,

in industrial societies the level at which an individual enters the work force is largely a function of vocational training and acquired occupational skills. These in turn depend partly on innate qualities and partly on the social ability (or inability) of an individual's family of origin to maximize those qualities through socialization, formal education and the transfer of inherited wealth. . . .[14]

Of course, some change in occupational structure, and in patterns of mobility, is inevitable as the society develops. If newcomers meet previously unmet needs and perform previously unknown tasks, they, rather than the native born, will predominate in certain rungs of the occupational ladder. Thus occupational mobility is also partly a function of the evolution of a society.

Occupational preferences are determined, in part, by culture—the values, traditions, beliefs, and institutions that are part of accumulated history. The trans-Atlantic crossing undoubtedly "uprooted" the Jewish immigrants who made the trip, but they still brought with them centuries of collective experience that eased their entry into Argentina. If necessity was the mother of invention for Jews in Argentina, tradition was the father.

BUENOS AIRES AND THE CHEVRAH

Where Jews lived in Buenos Aires was determined by preference within boundaries of necessity. The ghetto that Jews carved out provided both stability and jobs in the face of the chaotic forces of urban life.

When Jewish immigrants sought to create an institution to serve their community, they turned to the model they knew best, the Kehillah. In eastern Europe, the Kehillah had been a local self-governing body given a substantial degree of autonomy by the state, though in the final analysis the Kehillah was responsible to and dependent on national governments. The Kehillah reached its zenith in seventeenth-century Poland, but the system had its origins in medieval western Europe.[15] The archetypal Kehillah as it developed in Poland had a strong executive body composed of electors chosen from the membership. Democratic in intent, most eventually became oligarchal in fact, as elders, elected from among the wealthy and the learned, chose each other or passed the office along to their children. The elders received assistance from a paid staff of rabbis, judges, teachers, administrators, and inspectors. Voluntary associations affiliated with the Kehillah, each specializing in a particular community service, gave the middle class a voice in the organization.

In spite of its origins in religious matters, the Kehillah devoted most of its energies to civil concerns. It represented the community to the crown, and vice versa. Regulating every area of Jewish life, economic as well as spiritual, the Kehillah was often vulnerable to powerful internal and external pressures. Indebtedness meant raising new taxes, which provoked the wrath of the poor, who were forced to provide the bulk of the revenues. Eventually, class tensions impaired the ability of the Kehillah to work effectively, and Chasidism, the religious revival movement that spread through eastern Europe in the eighteenth century, led a majority of Jews to avoid the institution altogether.

The various partitions of Poland often subjected Jews to governments that perceived them as a problem. The monarchs of Prussia, Austria, and Russia believed that Jews had to be assimilated. The Russians abolished the Kehillah in 1844, although prominent Jews continued to be charged with such unpopular tasks as providing conscripts and tax revenues. In the face of such pressures, Jews closed ranks around the Kehillah and revived it. But only after the government had been served could the needs of the community be addressed. Again, class hostility toward those Jews who served the state surfaced, fueled by the ideologies of zionism and socialism, whose structure had little, if anything, to do with the Kehillah.

In spite of this tradition of fragmentation and class tensions, the Kehillah connoted for many Jews the idea of a time long past when Jews lived together harmoniously, providing for their own needs, more or less democratically, in largely self-contained communities. Such was the kind of community that Russian Jewish immigrants to Buenos Aires sought to reconstruct.

Of the hundreds of organizations, associations, and institutions that contributed to the cohesiveness of the Jewish community in Buenos Aires, none was more important than the Chevrah Keduscha Ashkenazi (CKA), which was established in 1895 to assure Jews, especially poor ones, proper burial according to tradition. Western European Jews played an important role in the Chevrah's early years, but they were gradually replaced by Ashkenazim. Because of its monopoly on funerals and its receipt of monthly dues, the Chevrah had comparatively greater resources at its disposal than any other Jewish voluntary association. It rapidly became the center of an extensive network of Jewish organizations and the institution that other associations and individuals looked to in time of need. It was not until 1949 that the Chevrah, reconstituting itself into the Asociación Mutual Israelita Argentina (AMIA), formally became a Kehillah, but it had been one in fact for half a century.

The history of the Chevrah's members is the story of ordinary people who lived anonymously and left little to posterity. Thus to write their history requires methods and techniques different from those on which historians usually rely. Using a variety of sources, the most

Table 1-1 : Data Available from Chevrah Records, 1905–1915[1]

Name	(Father's first name)	Marital Status	Age/membership Year of birth Year of death
Nationality	(at membership)		
Occupation	(at membership)	Nationality	(at time of death)
	(subsequent changes)	Month/year membership	
	(at time of death)	Address	(at membership)
Cause of death			(subsequent to membership)
			(at time of death)
		Place of death if not residence	

Survivors:

Name	Address	Occupation	Member of the AMIA?	Marital Status	Age

[1] Data available from the records of the Chevrah for the 1905–1910 and 1914–1915 samples. Note that occupations subsequent to membership were rarely reported, indicating that members either did not choose to report occupational changes or did not feel that their occupations had changed. Also, data on a member's survivors are available if the member died in or after 1949.

important of which are the records of the Chevrah Keduscha Ashkenazi, I have traced 1,514 eastern European Jews who emigrated to, or were born in, Argentina between 1890 and 1930. According to my calculations, between 85 and 95 percent of the community belonged to the Chevrah in the years before 1945. Some Jews preferred not to join, and the leadership barred others from membership, but the Chevrah did represent a valid cross section of the community.

To approximate the successive waves of eastern European Jewish immigration to Argentina, I drew six random samples, one from the census (in manuscript form) of 1895, and five from the Chevrah's membership records. Each sample relates to specific stage in the histories of eastern Europe and Argentina. Tables 1-1 and 1-2 give the data available for the five samples taken from the records of the Chevrah. Table 1-3 shows the maximum amount of information obtainable from the Chevrah's records.

The group of Jews present in Buenos Aires in 1895 were pioneers, many of whom traveled from Russia to England, France, or Austria and then to Argentina, others of whom went from Buenos Aires to the

Table 1-2 : Data Available from Chevrah Records, 1920–1930[1]

Name	(Father's first name)	*Marital Status*	*Age/membership*
			Year of birth
Nationality	(at membership)		*Year of death*
Occupation	(prior to membership)	*Change in Nationality*	
		Month/year of membership	
	(at membership)		
		Address	(prior to membership)
	(at time of death)	*Length of Residence*	
		(at time of membership)	
Number of years in Argentina			
		Length of Residence	
Number of family members		(subsequent to	
		membership)	
Number of males (by age)			
		(at time of death)	
Number of females (by age)			
		Place of death if not residence	
Relatives in the AMIA?			
		Cause of death	
Member of other associations?			
Which?			

Survivors:

Name	Address	Occupation	*Member of the AMIA?*	*Marital Status*	Age

[1] Data available from the records of the Chevrah for the 1920, 1925, and 1930 samples.

colonies or the interior and then returned. These early inhabitants laid the foundation for the community's institutional structure, helped to define its occupational patterns, and founded a neighborhood in which later immigrants would live.

The 1905–1910 sample reflects the influence of immigration at the turn of the century as well as immigration stimulated by the pogroms of 1903, the Russo-Japanese War, and the Russian revolution of 1905. Unfortunately, the scarcity of data for this and the subsequent sample, 1914–1915, hides many aspects of these people's lives from us. The 1914–1915 sample includes refugees from the economic and religious persecutions of Tsar Nicholas II and some who arrived about the beginning of World War I.

The fourth sample, 1920, includes those who emigrated during wartime as well as the first wave of postwar immigrants. Changes in the Chevrah's keeping of records in 1918 permit for the first time a relatively complete view of family size, previous occupations, residential patterns, and other variables. The 1925 sample represents the Soviet

Table 1-3 : Maximum Data Available from Chevrah Records[1]

Name	(Father's first name)	*Marital Status*	*Age/membership* *Year of birth* *Year of death*
Nationality	(at membership)		
Change in nationality *Year of naturalization*		*Month/year membership*	
Occupation	(prior to membership)	*Address* *Length of Residence*	(prior to membership)
	(at membership)	(at time of membership)	
	(subsequent changes)	*Length of Residence*	(subsequent to membership)
	(at time of death)		(at time of death)
Number of years in Argentina			
Number of family members		*Place of death if not residence*	
Number of males (by age)			
Number of females (by age)		Address of work place in 1917, 1921, 1927, 1936, 1945	
Relatives in the AMIA?			
Member of other associations? *Which?*		Membership in other associations subsequent to membership	
Occupation in 1895, 1917, 1921, 1927, 1936, 1945		Literate? Going to school? Owns real property?	
Number of business locations		Size and type of estate	
In business with (relationship of partner, type of partnership)			

Survivors:

Name	Address	Occupation	Member of the AMIA?	Marital Status	Age

[1]The maximum amount of data available from the records of the Chevrah. These data are not all available for every member of every sample.

regime's hardening position on immigration and the increasingly harsh conditions that Jews faced in postwar Poland. Polish Jews began to arrive in Buenos Aires in large numbers about this time, a trend that surfaces in this sample. The final sample, 1930, is composed largely of immigrants who arrived in the 1920s. It contains the largest number of Poles and the highest percentage of native-born Argentines.[16]

Notes

1. United States, House of Representatives, *Executive Documents for the Fifty-Second Congress, 1891–1892*, Vol. I (Washington: Government Printing Office, 1892), p. 56.

2. *Jewish Chronicle*, May 13, 1887, and *Jewish Chronicle*, August 5, 1887.

3. For examples of the community's historiography, see: "Di Presse," *Argentina: veinte años de "Di Presse"* (Buenos Aires: Di Presse, 1938); Hirsch Triwaks ed., *Cincuenta años de vida judía en la Argentina* (Buenos Aires: Talleres Graficos, Julio Glassman, 1940); and Delegación de Asociaciones Israelitas Argentinas, *Cincuenta años de colonización judía en la Argentina* (Buenos Aires: Di Presse, 1939); Boleslao Lewin, *El judío en la época colonial* (Buenos Aires: Colegio Libre de Estudios Superiores, 1939). The phrase "gauchos judíos" is Alberto Gerchunoff's. See: Alberto Gerchunoff, *Los gauchos judíos* (Buenos Aires: Editorial Universitaria de Buenos Aires, 1964). For studies of the Jewish Agricultural colonies, see: S. Hurvitz, *Colonia Lucienville* (Buenos Aires: 1932), in Yiddish; Gregorio Verbitzky, *Rivera: afán de medio siglo* (Buenos Aires: Comisión del cincuentario de Rivera, 1955); Morton D. Winsberg, *Colonia Baron Hirsch* (Gainesville: University of Florida Press, 1963); and José Liebermann, *Tierra soñada* (Buenos Aires: Luis Lasserre y Cia, 1959). Also see: Martin A. Cohen, ed., *The Jewish Experience in Latin America*, 2 vols. (Waltham: American Jewish Historical Society, 1971).

4. Lucien Wolf, "The New Moses," *London Daily Graphic*, July 7, 1894.

5. Quoted in, Samuel J. Lee, *Moses of the New World* (New York: Thomas Yoscloff, 1970), p. 263.

6. James Scobie, *Argentina: A City and a Nation* 2nd ed. (New York: Oxford University Press, 1970), pp. 160–161.

7. **Argentine Population Growth, 1869–1947**

Year	Population[1]	Percent Urban[2]
1869	1,830,000	25
1895	4,045,000	37
1914	7,885,000	53
1947	15,894,000	63

Notes: [1]*Rounded off.*
[2]Urban is defined as towns above 2,000 people.

Source: National censuses of 1869, 1895, 1914, and 1947.

Population Growth of Buenos Aires and Metropolitan Buenos Aires, 1895–1947 and Percent of Total Argentine Population[1]

Year	Buenos Aires	Percent	Metro. Buenos Aires	Percent
1895	656	16.2	774	19.1
1904	945	18.5	1,133	22.0
1914	1,561	20.0	2,019	25.8
1924	1,839	18.5	2,439	25.2
1930	2,287	19.5	3,087	26.3
1938	2,463	18.0	3,628	26.4
1947	2,981	19.0	4,722	29.9

Note: [1] In thousands.
Source: Charles S. Sargent, *The Spatial Evolution of Greater Buenos Aires, Argentina, 1870–1930.* (Tempe: Arizona State University Press, 1974) p. 146.

8. *Jewish Chronicle,* July 24, 1908, and Jewish Colonization Association, *Rapport,* 1980, p. 15 and Jewish Colonization Association, *Rapport,* 1909, p. 12.

9.   **Estimates of the Jewish Population of Argentina, 1920–1936**

Year	Weill	Rosenswaike[1]
1920	126,927	120,000
1921	130,901	123,612
1922	136,772	129,049
1923	145,306	137,283
1924	161,186	151,330
1925	171,403	160,424
1926	180,894	168,885
1927	191,140	177,503
1928	199,590	184,519
1929	209,396	192,693
1930	218,523	200,423
1931	229,605	229,605
1932	236,602	214,579
1933	241,952	218,501
1934	247,544	222,403
1935	253,471	226,565
1936	260,432	230,595

Note: [1] For a critique of Weill's computations, see: Ira Rosenswaike, "The Jewish Population of Argentina," p. 211.
Source: Simon Weill, *Población Israelita en la República Argentina* (Buenos Aires: Bene Berith, 1936), pp. 28–29.

Ira Rosenswaike, "The Jewish Population of Argentina: Census and Estimates, 1887–1947," *Jewish Social Studies,* 22 (October 1960), pp. 195–214.

10. Gino Germani, "Mass Immigration and Modernization in Argentina," in I. L. Horowitz, ed., *Masses in Latin America* (New York: Oxford University Press, 1970), pp. 303, 305 and 322.

11. Ricardo Levene, *A History of Argentina*. Trans. and ed. William Spence Robertson (Chapel Hill: University of North Carolina Press, 1937), p. 517.

12. See: Walter Little, "Political Integration in Peronist Argentina" (Cambridge, unpublished dissertation, Cambridge University, 1971). See also: David Rock, *Politics in Argentina, 1890–1930* (London: Cambridge University Press, 1975) and Rock's "Radicalism and the Urban Working Classes in Argentina, 1916–1922" (Cambridge: unpublished dissertation, Cambridge University, 1971).

13. Stephan Thernstrom, "The Dimensions of Occupational Mobility," Robert P. Swierenga, ed., *Quantification in American History* (New York: Atheneum, 1970), p. 369.

14. Leonard Broom and F. Lancaster Jones, "Career Mobility in Three Societies: Australia, Italy, and the United States," *American Sociological Review,* 34 (October 1969), 652.

15. For the historical development of such institutions, see: Michael Zarchin, *Jews in the Province of Posen* (Philadelphia: Dropsie College, 1939).

16. Chevrah records reflect traditional Jewish patriarchalism and prevented an examination of the role of women in the community. For the role of women in the immigrant experience see, among others: Virginia Yans-McLaughlin, "Like the Fingers of the Hand: The Family and Community Life of First Generation Italian-Americans in Buffalo, New York, 1890–1930," (Buffalo, unpublished dissertation, State University of New York at Buffalo, 1970) and Virginia Yans-McLaughlin, "A Flexible Tradition: South Italian Immigrants Confront a New Work Experience," *Journal of Social History,* 7 (Summer 1974), 429–445.

THE PALE

When in 1882 an Odessa cantor chanted "all the nations reside on their land, but Israel wanders the earth like a shadow finding no rest, receiving no brotherly welcome," his congregants audibly sobbed.[1] The more than five million Jews of Russia needed no reminder that they had been ruled by a dynasty of tsars dedicated to their destruction, assimilation, or emigration—that life was a succession of persecution, economic disability, and political discrimination. The mass of Russian Jews endured poverty, degradation, and humiliation. Only their traditions, institutions, and values provided enough cohesiveness for the Jewish communities of eastern Europe to withstand the onslaught of tsarist autocracy.

THE TSARIST LEGACY

The reforms instituted in the 1860s by Alexander II, the "Tsar Liberator," who freed the serfs, eased Jewish disabilities, and set Russia on a modernizing course by nurturing the development of an increasingly complex social structure in Russia. Underdeveloped prior to the abolition of serfdom in 1861, Russia slowly began to industrialize after the ties that bound millions of peasants to the soil were severed. Railroads began to crisscross the land, and former serfs migrated to cities. National income rose, and infusions of foreign capital brought some prosperity to Russia, which expanded economically into both Europe and Asia.[2] Gradually an industrial working class began to grow, as did an internal market capable of supporting an industrial economy.

A handful of Jews benefited from this expansion of the Russian economy. Especially in railroad construction and contracting, banking, finance, and insurance, a small Jewish "plutocracy" evolved. These Jews employed others in managerial and sales positions and fostered

15

the growth of a Jewish middle class in the larger interior cities, especially Moscow and St. Petersburg.[3]

But this Jewish bourgeoisie amounted to only a tiny fraction of the total Jewish population. Although it possessed some economic power, its ability to influence policy was limited. Wealthy Jews proved incapable of wielding enough power to improve the lives of their poverty-stricken coreligionists.[4]

Before abolition, and to a lesser degree after it, Jewish artisans produced goods for peasants who had limited incomes and equally limited needs. The goods produced, the techniques of their production, and the quality of life of the producers were primitive.[5]

Most Russian Jews lived in a region called the Pale of Settlement, consisting of 362,000 square miles and including portions of Poland, Lithuania, White Russia, southwestern Russia, and southern Russia. When the tsar's government censused the empire in 1897, it counted 5,215,805 people who claimed to be Jewish, 94 percent of whom lived in the Pale. Only 4 percent lived in the interior provinces, which included Moscow and St. Petersburg, and 2 percent lived in Asiatic Russia. Despite their concentration, even within the Pale Jews were a minority of the population, albeit a growing one.

Demographic pressures in the empire during the last half of the nineteenth century helped produce hostile relations between Jews and non-Jews, with both groups competing for scarce resources. In spite of the modernization beginning in the 1860s, Russia's economy could not support so rapidly growing a population. Between 1850 and 1900, the Jewish population of Russia tripled, and in the two decades after 1880, when anti-Jewish measures stimulated emigration, the Jewish population still increased by a quarter. Cities expanded, and the Jewish population in urban areas grew. Between 1855 and 1860, approximately one Jew in ten lived in a city of more than 10,000 people; by 1900 almost 25 percent lived in such cities. Jews constituted almost 38 percent of the urban population in the Pale in 1897 and 80 percent of the Jews in the Pale lived in urban areas.[6]

A series of legal restrictions in the last two decades of the century worsened population pressures. In May 1882, slightly more than one year after his father was assassinated, Tsar Alexander III promulgated the originally temporary May Laws (in effect until 1917), which forbade Jews from settling in villages on the outskirts of cities and towns, from acquiring real property in rural areas, and from conducting business on Sundays and on Christian holidays. Urban Jews had no choice but to remain in cities, and rural Jews were forced into urban areas.

The territory in which Jews could legally reside was thus reduced by 90 percent. Other laws limited educational opportunities and barred Jews from government offices.[7]

Following a near fatal railroad accident in 1888, the tsar, obeying what he believed to be God's will, intensified his efforts at counter-reform. These restrictions—only the more important of which are considered here—were imposed in an ever more hostile atmosphere. Provincial authorities further reduced the territory open to Jewish settlement by redefining towns and townlets into villages which, considered rural, were barred to Jews. Jews who had settled in those areas after 1882 were expelled from them. Alexander III closed a 30-mile deep stretch of Russia's western border to Jews, further inflating population densities within the Pale.

As Alexander III's regime became more overtly hostile toward Jews, pogroms became more frequent. These attacks on people and property varied in severity and affected different Jews in different ways. Simon Dubnow, the great historian of Russian Jewry, noted that during one typical pogrom "the riots resulted in some two hundred ruined houses and stores in the outskirts of town, where the Jewish proletariat was cooped up. The central part of town, where the more well-to-do Jews had their residences, was guarded by the police and by a military detachment, and therefore remained intact."[8]

Nor were the May laws and pogroms the extent of it. Those Jewish artisans permitted to live outside the Pale could neither change occupations nor sell products not of their own making, important obstacles to capital accumulation and social mobility. In the Pale, schools admitted Jews in a one-to-ten ratio to Christians, while outside it laws restricted Jews to 5 percent of the admissions. In Moscow and St. Petersburg, Jews were allowed only 3 percent of all school seats.

In 1891, the regime expelled Jews from St. Petersburg and Moscow altogether. According to Dubnow, "people who had lived in Moscow for twenty, thirty, and even forty years were forced to sell their property . . . and leave the city. Those who were too poor to comply with the orders of the police or did not succeed in selling their property for a mere song—there were cases of poor people disposing of their whole furniture for one or two rubles—were thrown into jail, or sent to transportation prison. . . . In this way some 20,000 Jews who had lived in Moscow . . . were forcibly removed to the Jewish Pale of Settlement."[9] It was in this context that the Russian government began to negotiate with Baron Hirsch to facilitate the exodus of some three million Jews from Russia.

THE LAST OF THE TSARS

The little-loved Alexander III died in November 1894. Leon Trotsky attributed his own revolutionary fervor to "the conditions existing under the reign of Alexander III; the high-handedness of police; the exploitation practiced by the landlords; the grafting by officials; the nationalistic restrictions; and in general, the entire social atmosphere of the time."[10]

One need look no further than Trotsky's own life struggle to know that Nicholas II was no better than his father. To Dubnow, the last Romanoff was "the most gloomy and reactionary of all. A man of limited intelligence, he attempted to play the role of an unlimited autocrat, fighting in blind rage against the cause of liberty."[11] The new tsar retained his father's advisors, including the infamous Pobedonostev, who so succinctly defined Russian policy on the Jewish question: "one third will die out, one third will leave the country, and one third will be completely dissolved in the surrounding population."[12]

The net effect of Nicholas II's policies was to bring about the complete economic collapse of Russian Jewry. The introduction of a state liquor monopoly, for example, ruined hundreds of thousands of Jews employed in the sale and distribution of alcohol as well as those who kept hotels and inns. Poverty and pauperism among Jews increased so dramatically that even non-Jewish Russian economists began to focus their attention on the state of Jews in Russia.

The Russian census of 1897 determined that almost one-third of all gainfully employed Jews participated in some form of commerce. Within the Pale, 75 percent of all merchants were Jewish, about half of them in agriculture (in cattle or grain dealing, for example). Another quarter served as middlemen and peddlers. Jews figured most prominently in the least lucrative branches of commerce and survived because they accepted profits that were lower than the prevailing rates. Industralization, increased competition, and urbanization all worsened the economic standing of the petty merchant, pushing many Jewish businessmen from commerce into the trades or factories. To be sure, relatively few Jews ever became wealthy in commerce. The regime's own Pahlen Commission noted that, despite their numerical superiority in the commercial sector, Jews controlled less than half of all commerce in the Pale. The line separating merchants from workers was perilously thin, and it was often crossed.

By the end of the nineteenth century, Jews accounted for between two-thirds and three-quarters of the artisans within the Pale, making up about 33 percent of the total working Jewish population. Of these artisans, some 260,000 were masters, 141,000 were journeymen, and 102,000 were apprentices. Because masters worked for other masters or for middlemen, almost half were wage earners, concentrated most heavily in the clothing industry; this was a pattern Jews would maintain in the countries to which they emigrated.[13]

Traditionally, to be a Jewish artisan meant owning a small establishment and relying either on one's family or a few journeymen or apprentices for labor. Artisans marketed their products in a variety of ways, depending on the vagaries of Russian industrialization. In some cases, tailors would visit peasant villages once a week. During these visits, they lived with their customers and brought their own pots in which to cook kosher food. Paid in food or by the job, which rarely amounted to more than a ruble, these tailors relied on thimbles and thread, not sewing machines. Some shoemakers worked in orchards during the summer, when many villagers went barefoot, to augment their incomes.[14] As the number of peasants declined, some Jewish artisans began to sell at markets or fairs. Others worked, permanently or temporarily, for middlemen. In one small town, for example, 500 weavers of talesim (prayer shawls) sold to three or four intermediaries who then distributed the product throughout the Pale.[15]

Even in larger towns and cities, the average workshop consisted of only two people—the master and an assistant. The journeyman often became a regular member of the household (indeed, a single man from another town might well live with his employer), but was frequently exploited. Still, as Ezra Mendelsohn relates, in spite of this arbitrary treatment "it should be emphasized that the Jewish journeyman by no means considered himself permanently a wage earner. As he saw it, were he compelled to suffer the insults of his master one day, the next he might himself become an employer, the master of his own shop."[16] In certain trades, the absence of clear-cut distinctions between employer and employee complicated the situation. Bundist leaders recognized that "since many Jewish artisans might in time become employers who could operate independently within their own shops 'a worker regards his situation as temporary and agrees to put up with a certain amount of sacrifice.' "[17] Even in Russia, the nature of the occupational structure, and of the trades themselves, produced a certain amount of occupational mobility.

The larger the establishment, the more rigid was the distinction between worker and owner. As the speed of Russian industralization accelerated, factories replaced individual artisans and proletarianized them. The case of the carpenters of Vilna, who after 1905 could no longer "regard themselves as future employers; [but] have become permanently hired laborers," was repeated in every major Lithuanian city and probably in every industralizing city in the Pale.[18] Store owners with larger demands replaced individual customers. By the turn of the century, for instance, master carpenters depended entirely upon the furniture store owners for whom they worked. Increasingly, master craftsmen were masters in name only.

These alterations in the production and sale of merchandise did little to improve the standard of living of journeymen or apprentices. Hours were long and wages pitifully low. Thus "a journeyman was expected to work 'without limit,' which usually meant from sunrise to sunset, while on Saturdays, after the Sabbath rest, and on Thursdays as well, his work extended into the early morning hours." In Vitebsk the workday was between thirteen and eighteen hours long; while in Gomel tailors, joiners, locksmiths, and shoemakers all worked between sixteen and eighteen hours a day.[19] Income remained low because many craftsmen depended on piecework and were paid irregularly. Usually work was available only during part of the year. Thus coatmakers might earn weekly wages during the winter but nothing during warm weather. The workers in Minsk who said that "from ten weeks of work we must live fifty-two weeks" spoke for hundreds of thousands of Jewish workers.[20]

Most artisans lived in squalor. Aaron Liebermann, a pioneer in the Jewish socialist movement, noted that Jewish workers "lived in the semi-darkness of cellars and similar hovels that had wet walls and floors, and were crammed together in an oppressive, stupefying atmosphere."[21] Another observer remarked that "the homes of the artisans are small and crowded. But no matter how small and crowded, tenants are often admitted, and there is seldom more than one room for a family. The room serves as a kitchen, living and sleeping room, and workshop."[22] Jacob Lestchinsky summed up the general situation when he wrote that "destitution, poverty and privation, need and hunger, in the fullest meaning of the word, sweating-system, shrunk chests, lifeless eyes, pale faces, sick and tubercular lungs—this is the picture of the Jewish street. . . . Is it surprising that he who can deserts the Jewish street, escapes where is he able to find a refuge?"[23]

Taxation represented another significant problem for Russia's Jews. As urban residents they paid high, indirect levies that increased by almost 110 percent between 1880 and 1901. Taxes specifically aimed at the Jewish community also forced many Jews closer to the margin. For example, the "box tax," collected on kosher meat, was introduced in 1844 to meet expenditures for Jewish community needs. The historian Jacob Frumkin explained that "the city councils were empowered to confer with 'resident and well to do Jews' concerning the allocation of box tax funds. . . . Although the sums obtained [were] to be used solely for Jewish needs, they were frequently applied to purposes which had nothing to do with Jewish life."[24] Leo Errera, who visited Russia in the early 1890s, reported that "the Jews also pay special taxes on house rent, on shops, on warehouses, on the income of factories, and on the various industrial or commercial enterprises which belong to them; whilst their printing presses, and the capital bequeathed by them, are all and each burdened by exorbitant taxation."[25] Colonel John Weber, an investigator from the United States, estimated that Jews paid taxes of 230,000 rubles on Sabbath candles alone.[26] The effect was to exacerbate not only local economic woes but class tensions as well.

Charitable and voluntary associations, often organized by trade, proliferated in an attempt to stem the omnipresent poverty of Russian Jewry. Theirs was, at best, a stopgap effort. Between 1894 and 1898, the number of Jewish families requiring charitable assistance increased some 27 percent. In 1897, a number of cities reported that more than half of their Jewish inhabitants were unemployed. During Passover of that year, between 40 and 50 percent of the Jewish population of such cities as Odessa, Vilna, Minsk, and Kovno received assistance. According to the Jewish Colonization Association, about 700,000 Jews applied for relief in 1898. While the unskilled were hardest hit, a large number of retail merchants and artisans were also affected.[27]

Karl Kautsky, the German Social Democrat, wrote in 1901 that ". . . if the Russian proletariat is more exploited than any other proletariat, there exists yet another class of workers who are still more oppressed, exploited, and ill-treated than all the others; this pariah among pariahs is the Jewish proletariat in Russia."[28] This situation, too, was a cost of modernization and industrialization. Jewish artisans had entered a state of irreversible downward mobility. Their workmanship was poor, and because of a lack of capital they were unable to take advantage of technological improvements. They found themselves in an uncompetitive position with respect to both factories and peasant handicrafts. This inability to eke out a livelihood accounts for the large number of emigrating artisans and skilled wage workers.

Bleak futures also existed for Jewish workers in large industrial centers like Lodz and Bialystok, textile boom towns that housed large numbers of Jewish factory workers. Working either in small factories or in cottage industries, these workers fell outside the scope of Russian labor legislation and were at the mercy of their employers, most of whom were also Jewish.[29] As Yiddish poet Abraham Liessen noted, in the West and in the industrial zones of Russia "workers struggle against capitalists who are very wealthy, while in our Jewish towns and cities the workers struggle against people like themselves."[30] Jewish-owned factories were labor rather than capital intensive, and even the largest of them employed an average of only twenty-five workers. Only in factories that produced cigarettes and matches could Jewish establishments compete with non-Jewish ones in terms of size. And even in those cases, machine power was rare and the work, performed mostly by women and children, was poorly remunerated. Still, skilled workers fared far better than the unskilled.

An 1897 report by the Jewish Colonization Association counted some 100,000 unskilled Jewish workers but omitted data from several large cities. It is safe to assume that about one tenth of the employed Jewish population lacked skills. Wages for this sector surpassed those paid in agriculture, but both types of workers bordered on pauperism.[31]

Unskilled workers were also jolted by modernization. Inefficient processes and workers were replaced by more modern techniques and inventions. Wages were uniformly low but varied with job, location, time of year, and whether workers received board.

Economic depression ushered out the nineteenth century in Russia. The slump began when a series of international crises caused a severe shortage of capital, a curtailment of railroad construction, and a reduction in state orders from heavy industry. The textile industry, in which Jews figured prominently, was also hard hit. A report from Lodz described the pall over the city in 1900: "One need only to walk down Petrovskaia street . . . to see how many victims there are. . . . Yes, all these gentlemen bustling about . . . are people who have closed down or are closing down factories and small workshops; . . . And where did the workers go when the factories closed down? They went nowhere; they, too, crowd the streets of Lodz. More than 2,000 men with families are registered with the bureau set up by the Jewish Philanthropic Society which seeks to alleviate their lot."[32]

The following year, the economy reached a new low, and full recovery remained a dim hope. In this setting of economic dispair, pogroms became more frequent and more brutal. The worst of them took place in Kishineff in 1903 and provoked an angry international response. Undaunted, the regime instigated other pogroms, believing that they stifled revolutionary (synonymous, so thought Russia's leaders, with Jewish) activity. From 1903 on, anti-Semitism became inexorably linked to the tsar's domestic and foreign policies.

In the aftermath of the 1905 Revolution, Jews unsuccessfully renewed their efforts to secure human rights. Their requests fell on deaf ears as the tsar responded to revolutionary movements, and the alleged Jewish masterminds behind the insurrection, with more repression. As the tide of revolution rose, reaction became more generalized. In 1910, the regime expelled Jews from villages within the Pale and from cities outside it. Meanwhile, the economic health of the Jewish community in Russia remained critical, as oppression, revolution, and finally world war and its associated horrors struck the empire.

The outbreak of World War I did not soften the regime's treatment of Jews. During the war, entire Jewish communities were transferred from one part of the empire to another, with pogroms accompanying the retreat of the tsar's forces from Galicia, Lithuania, and Poland. It was only with the success of the Russian Revolution in 1917 that the legal and political status of the Jews in Russia finally began to improve.

THE POLISH EXPERIENCE

World War I had important consequences for the Jews of eastern Europe. In addition to the Bolshevik Revolution, it set in motion a number of independence movements, and by war's end a new balance of power existed in the area. Poland became independent for the first time since 1795, reconstructing itself from the defeated empires of the Central Powers to the west and from the Soviet Union to the east. Rumania received new territory, while Lithuania, also a major center of eastern European Jewish life, became a pawn in a larger game between Russia and Poland.

For more than a century, the history of Polish Jewry had been synonymous with that of Russian Jewry. Particularly after the abortive revolt for independence in 1863, the tsar firmly controlled Jewish policy in Poland.

The abolition of serfdom notwithstanding, Polish industrial development proceeded slowly, and in 1914 about 75 percent of the population still lived as peasants. As in Russia, the majority of Jews worked in commerce or in petty production; three of every four people so occupied were Jewish. The spread of capitalism adversely affected Polish Jews, just as it did their coreligionists in Russia. The growth of modern banking, the need for credit, more and larger units of production, all contributed to the economic insecurity of the petty bourgeoisie and to the marginalization of the artisan. In addition to these more widespread economic trends, Jews also suffered from legal discrimination, politically inspired violence, and the linkage of anti-Semitism and antisocialism. Both the traditional ruling class and the rising, industrially based elite recognized that anti-Semitism could deflect social protest from the real issues.[33]

Postwar Poland was in desperate straits, partly because the wartime occupation of the country had resulted in the destruction of vital industries and machinery. In Lodz, the German army stripped machines of essential leather and copper. The loss of a Russian market for Poland's textiles and clothing industries also hurt the country.

If, before the war, life was a struggle for the mass of Polish Jewry, the situation during and after the war was even worse. The German government deported more than 600,000 Jews and Poles to work in its war industries.[34] The last years of the war also saw a series of major and minor violent attacks on Polish Jews. Henry Morgenthau's 1919 report, commissioned to investigate allegations of anti-Semitism in the country, stated that "the result of all these minor persecutions is to keep the Jewish population in a state of ferment, and to subject them to the fear that graver excesses may again occur." Commenting on the economic crisis of Poland's Jews, Morgenthau wrote, "the economic condition of Poland is at its lowest ebb. Manufacturing and commerce have virtually ceased. The shortage, the high price, and the imperfect distribution of food are a dangerous menace to the health and welfare of the urban population. As a result, hundreds of thousands are suffering from hunger and are but half-clad, while thousands are dying of disease and starvation. The cessation of commerce is particularly felt in the Jewish population, who are almost entirely dependent upon it."[35] A significant proportion of Polish Jewry lived on contributions from abroad.

Poland emerged from the war an independent nation of 27 million people of whom eight percent were Jews. The second largest Polish minority, Jews increased rapidly in number; by 1931, in spite of significant emigration, more than three million people identified themselves as Jews. One contemporary noted that "as in other countries the large majority of them are very poor, suffering severely from hunger and privation. Want of employment is prevalent, although a large proportion of them are artisans and labourers."[36] As in Russia, most Polish Jews earned their living in petty commerce or as workers "in cheap furniture, clothes, and leather, but inferior in skill to the Poles; and in other trades, too, but always tending to unskilled labor."[37]

Unlike the majority of Poles, most Jews lived in cities, and by 1921 they formed absolute majorities in ten cities with populations between 20,000 and 50,000. Jews accounted for one of every three people in Warsaw. In most urban areas, "the East Jew is not only the prosperous business man, he is the slum dweller, living in unimaginable squalor and poverty, and occupying almost all the slums."[38]

The Polish government's abandonment of laissez-faire policies and active participation in the economy contributed to the deprivation of the Poland's Jews. The state became the primary employer, the leading entrepreneur, the controller of credit and tariffs, and the tax collector. In these efforts it usually sought to advance the interests of the Polish majority against ethnic minorities. The government barred Jews from employment in state enterprises and forced them out of many professions. It gave minimal support to Hebrew or Yiddish schools, which declined in number as financing them became impossible for Jewish communities.

Because of the growing success of an economic boycott of Jewish businesses, which had started in 1912 but which had faltered when the war made everything scarce, the percentage of Jews employed in manufacturing rose between 1921 and 1931 while that of Jews in trade fell.[39] A government policy that encouraged the migration of peasants to cities also affected Jews adversely. In eastern Poland, for instance, the number of Jewish business establishments declined by almost 60 percent while the number of non-Jewish businesses increased by 40 percent. The only licenses Jews found readily obtainable were those for hawking and peddling, the least desirable forms of commerce. The desperate straits of the Jewish community were obvious to Horace Kallen, an American who visited Poland in the mid-1920s. He wrote that "robots asking for bread and receiving a prayer may be set down as a not inadequate description of 'them.' 'Them' are the mass of Polish Jews; . . . they are becoming . . . more and more outcasts of its economy." During Kallen's trip "more than half of the Jewish laborers, skilled and unskilled were out of work. The rest were employed more or less."[40]

More than 80 percent of working-class Jews were employed in artisan's workshops or in very small factories. The overwhelming majority in business for themselves depended either on one hired helper or on free family labor. On the average, Jewish factory workers earned money only during sixteen to twenty-two weeks of the year. Those who worked alone, on the other hand, averaged eight months of employment but earned less money.[41] Both unemployed and underemployment were constant spectres in the Jewish sections of Poland.

Independence brought Jews little relief. Legal restrictions remained and helped to accelerate the precipitous economic decline of Polish Jewry. By 1934, one in every four Polish Jews received some form of charity. In Warsaw, the percentage of those receiving aid rose from 22 percent in 1934 to 60 percent in 1935. Estimates of the number of Jews living in poverty and destitution ranged between 80 and 90 percent of the total Jewish population.[42]

THE RUMANIAN EXPERIENCE

Rumania's 200,000 Jews, meanwhile, were affected by the same problems that plagued minorities throughout central Europe. Discriminatory practices leveled at other minorities were directed more severely toward Jews. The development of capitalism and the efforts of a new ruling class to build a modern state also caused severe dislocations in traditional patterns of life for Rumanian Jews. As was happening in Russia and Poland, the Rumanian elite used anti-Semitism to attack Jews in commerce, finance, and manufacturing, hoping in this way to deflect the anger of a restless peasantry.

From the middle of the nineteenth century until the Rumanian Jewish community was destroyed during the Second World War, successive regimes relied on anti-Semitism to maintain power. They disregarded the protests of concerned governments and private organizations in the West and continued, overtly or through subterfuge, to support discriminatory policies that would stimulate Jewish emigration. Special legislation directed against Jews prevented them from purchasing real estate in towns, forced them to pay for the same education that Rumanians received for free, and either barred Jews from secondary schools or admitted them under rigid quotas. Jews could not practice law, work on railroads, peddle, hawk, or lend money.[43]

It was not surprising, therefore, that between 1871 and 1914 nearly 30 percent of all Rumanian Jews emigrated to the Americas. The so-called "Rumanian exodus" began in earnest in 1889, when poor harvests triggered a severe depression and prompted the government to strictly enforce anti-Semitic laws that denied Jews jobs of almost any kind.

Like their coreligionists in Russia and Poland, most Jews were poor. Skilled laborers and petty traders, they were increasingly marginalized by modernization and by exclusionary legislation. The Bucharest Society of Jewish Artisans succinctly summarized the feelings of most Rumanian Jews this way: "Countless laws were promulgated against us. Ostensibly, these are laws against foreigners, but in effect they are applied to us. We, natives of this land, are treated like unpro-

tected foreigners. . . . And when we do dare to protest, we are answered with pogroms. . . . We want to live like human beings, and if
this is impossible here, we shall live elsewhere."[44]

Most of those who emigrated went to the United States or Canada,
but others were routed to Argentina so as not to antagonize U.S.
immigration officials worried about an unending stream of eastern
European Jews.[45] Because of the reluctance of Jewish agencies to
organize and support this potentially disruptive emigration from Rumania, most of it occurred spontaneously.

When, in 1902, the United States intervened to prevent the emigration of those it regarded as undesirable wards, Secretary of State Hay
wrote of the Rumanian Jews that they

> are prohibited from owning land, or even from cultivating it as common
> laborers. They are debarred from residing in rural districts. Many
> branches of petty trade and manual production are closed to them in the
> overcrowded cities where they are forced to dwell and engage, against
> fearful odds, in the desperate struggle for existence. Even as ordinary
> artisans they may find employment in the proportion of one 'unprotected
> alien' to two 'Rumanians' under any one employer. In short, by the
> cumulative effect of successive restrictions, the Jews of Rumania have
> become reduced to a state of wretched misery.[46]

TOWARD A NEW HOME

Several factors led millions of Jews to leave eastern Europe. The
economic deterioration of their communities, ghettoization, occupational marginalization, legal and political discrimination, and pogroms
all contributed to the vast population movement. The flight of Jews
from poverty and persecution was, of course, part of a much larger
process in which the poor of Europe roamed the world in search of
economic security, political freedom, and religious toleration. That
they were willing to emigrate to lands of which they knew so little is
grim testimony to the wretchedness of what they left behind.

Why Jews chose to emigrate to Argentina in such large numbers
remains the subject of some speculation. Certainly, the desire of the
Argentine government to populate the pampa with Europeans who
would instill in native Argentines the values needed for economic and
social development played a part. According to such leaders as
Domingo F. Sarmiento, the most eloquent proponent of immigration,
only the European could instill civilization into the barbarous lands of

the gaucho. Also, the Conquest of the Desert, Argentina's equivalent to the extermination of the American Indian, greatly increased the pacified acreage under the government's control, creating a need for hardy settlers.

The Argentine government under President Julio A. Roca sought to attract Jews to settle and work the newly conquered territory. In 1882, Carlos Calvo, Argentine immigration commissioner in Paris, attempted to establish contacts that would induce Russian Jews to settle in Argentina. His efforts came to naught, partly because Jews still preferred the United States and Western Europe, and partly because the Roca plan aroused opposition within Argentina, some of it from Sarmiento himself.

Nearly a decade later, after reports attacking the myth of the United States as a "golden state" began to appear with some regularity in the European Jewish press, the emigration of Jews to Argentina began in earnest. Many Jews were ready to explore their alternatives; others cared not at all where they were going so long as they left eastern Europe. Still others, as we have seen, believed Buenos Aires a part of the United States. Throughout this period, the Jewish Colonization Association played an instrumental role in both bringing Argentina to the attention of countless Jews and in acting as a guarantor of their support while in the country. For its part, the Argentine government became more receptive to Jews when it realized that it would not have to support them.[47]

Notes

1. Louis Greenberg, *The Jews in Russia*, vol. II, (New Haven: Yale University Press, 1965), p. 55.

2. Nicholas V. Riasanovsky, *A History of Russia*, (New York: Oxford University Press, 1963) pp. 431–432.

3. Simon Dubnow, *History of the Jews in Russia and Poland*, vol. II, trans. I. Friedlander (Philadelphia: Jewish Publication Society, 1916–1920), p. 186. The phrase also appears in A. L. Patkin, *The Origins of the Russian Jewish Labor Movement* (Melbourne: F. W. Chesire, Ltd., 1947), p. 69.

4. Arcadius Kahan, "The Impact of the Industrialization Process in Tsarist Russia Upon the Socio-Economic Conditions of the Jewish Population (Observations and Comments)," paper read at UCLA, March 1972, p. 37.

5. *See:* Hirsch Abramovitch, "Rural Jewish Occupations in Lithuania," *YIVO Annual of Jewish Social Science*, vol. II–III (1948), 206–208.

6. I. M. Rubinow, "Economic Condition of the Jews in Russia," *Bulletin of the Bureau of Labor*, 15 (September 1907), 493.

7. *See:* Mark Vishniak, "Antisemitism in Tsarist Russia," ed. Koppel S. Pinson, *Essays on Antisemitism* (New York: Conference on Jewish Relations, 1946), pp. 79–110 and Leo Errera, *The Russian Jews* (London: David Nutt, 1894), pp. 13–14. I. M. Rubinow reported that "with the decline of the prosperity of the Russian and Polish nobility, the making of a living became more difficult for the Jew and this led to a moderate though unmistakable tendency to remove to the rural districts. Thither went the petty merchant, the liquor dealer, the artisan, and finally the prospective Jewish agriculturist," in "Economic Conditions of the Jews," p. 492.

8. Dubnow, *History of the Jews,* vol. II, p. 251.

9. Dubnow, *History of the Jews,* vol. II, pp. 405–406.

10. Leon Trotsky, "A Social Democrat Only," Lucy S. Dawidowicz, ed., *The Golden Tradition* (Boston: Beacon Press, 1967), p. 444.

11. Dubnow, *History of the Jews in Russia and Poland,* vol. III, p. 7.

12. Dubnow, *History of the Jews,* vol. III, p. 10. Variations of this quotation exist, but its essence is clear.

13. *See:* Rubinow, "Economic Condition of the Jews," pp. 520 and 523.

14. *See:* Hirsch Abramovitch, "Rural Jewish Occupations in Lithuania," *YIVO Annual of Jewish Social Science,* 2–3 (1948), 206–208.

15. Rubinow, "Economic Condition of the Jews," p. 525.

16. Ezra Mendelsohn, *Class Struggle in the Pale,* (London: Cambridge University Press, 1970), p. 9.

17. Irving Howe, *World of Our Fathers,* (New York: Harcourt, Brace, Jovanovich, 1976), p. 22.

18. Quoted by Mendelsohn, *Class Struggle,* p. 10. This trend was apparent as early as the 1890s.

19. Mendelsohn, *Class Struggle,* p. 11.

20. *See:* A. L. Patkin, *Origins of Russian Jewish Labor,* p. 40; Rubinow, "Economic Condition of the Jews," pp. 527–528; and Mendelsohn, *Class Struggle,* p. 11.

21. Aaron Liebermann, a pioneer in the Jewish socialist movement, quoted in Mendelsohn, *Class Struggle,* p. 13.

22. Rubinow, "Economic Condition of the Jews," p. 526.

23. Jacob Lestchinsky (spelled Leschczynski) quoted by Patkin, *Origins of Russian Jewish Labor,* p. 41.

24. In Jacob Frumkin, et al., *Russian Jewry, 1860–1917* (New York: Thomas Yoseloff, 1966), p. 23.

25. Errera stated "The Jews also pay special taxes on house rent, on shops, or warehouses, on the income of factories, and on the various industrial or commercial enterprises which belong to them: whilst their printing presses, and the capital bequeathed by them, are all and each burdened by exorbitant taxation," *The Russian Jews,* p. 98.

26. Theodore H. Von Laue, *Sergei Witte and the Industrialization of Russia* (New York: Atheneum, 1963), p. 101.

27. Rubinow, "Economic Condition of the Jews," p. 534.

28. Quoted by Mendelsohn, *Class Struggle,* p. 7.

29. The most frequently offered explanation of this phenomenon is that because Jews

would not work on Saturday and Christians would not work on Sunday, a mixed labor force would result in a five-day work week. Obviously, hiring only Jewish workers would also keep the factories running six days a week. Rather, it seems that Jews lacked the technical skills needed to operate modern looms. Also, and perhaps more importantly, employers felt that non-Jewish workers would be less likely to strike than their Jewish counterparts. Thus, the only jobs left to Jews (because non-Jewish factory owners did not hire Jews in number) were in small, primitive establishments that relied on manpower rather than horsepower. See: Mendelsohn, *Class Struggle,* pp. 20–23, and Rubinow, "Economic Condition of the Jews," p. 544.

30. Howe, *World of Our Fathers,* p. 22.

31. Rubinow, "Economic Condition of the Jews," p. 534.

32. M. I. Tugan-Baranovsky, *The Russian Factory in the 19th Century,* trans. Arthur and Clarora S. Levin (Homewood: Richard D. Irwin, 1970), p. 289.

33. Raphael Mahler, "Antisemitism in Poland," Koppel S. Pinson, ed., *Essays on Antisemitism,* pp. 111–114, 127. One Pole, linking the nineteenth century with industrialization, remarked, "There was never 19th century in Poland."

34. Arthur L. Goodhart, *Poland and the Minority Races* (London: George Allen & Unwin, 1920), p. 115 and Bernard K. Johnpoll, *The Politics of Futility* (Ithaca: Cornell University Press, 1967), p. 42.

35. National Polish Committee of America, "The Morgenthau Report," *The Jews in Poland: Official Reports of the American and British Investigating Missions* (Chicago: National Polish Committee of America, n.d.) p. 7.

36. Ibid, p. 8.

37. National Polish Committee of America, "The Samuels Report," *The Jews in Poland,* p. 23.

38. National Polish Committee of America, "The Captain Wright Report," *The Jews in Poland,* p. 36.

39. Jacob Lestchinsky, "The Industrial and Social Structure of the Jewish Population," *YIVO Annual of Jewish Social Science,* 11 (1956–1957), 247. Additional information also leads to the inescapable conclusion that "manufacture" means very small level production. One scholar wrote, "the Jewish workingmen of Poland were concentrated in an antiquated branch of production, a domestic system which was disintegrating in the face of a new industrialization, . . ." Joseph S. Roucek, "Minorities," Bernadotte E. Schmitt, ed., *Poland* (Berkeley: University of California Press, 1975), p. 160.

40. Horace M. Kallen, *Frontiers of Hope* (New York: Horace Liveright, 1929), pp. 194 and 197.

41. Jacob Lestchinsky, "The Jews in the Cities of the Republic of Poland" *YIVO Annual of Jewish Social Science,* 1 (1946), 156–177, 263. In 1937, the Polish Bund reported a total of 700,000 wage earners and 400,000 artisans among Poland's Jews. Cited in: Johnpoll, *The Politics of Futility,* p. 207.

42. William M. Glicksman, *In the Mirror of Literature,* (New York: Living Books, 1966), p. 61.

43. Zsombor de Szasz, *The Minorities in Roumanian Transylvania* (London: Richards Press, 1927), p. 332.

44. Joseph Kissman, "The Immigration of Rumanian Jews up to 1914," *YIVO Annual of Jewish Social Science,* 2–3 (1948), 168.

45. Zosa Szaikowski, "Jewish Emigration Policy in the Period of the Rumanian Exodus," *Jewish Social Studies,* 13 (January 1951), 47–70.

46. Note from John Hay to Charles S. Wilson, July 17, 1902, quoted in Cyrus Adler and Aaron M. Margalith, *American Intercession on Behalf of Jews in the Diplomatic Correspondence of the United States, (1840–1938)* (New York: American Jewish Historical Society, 1943), p. 124.

47. La Nación, *1891 Anuario La Nación,* (Buenos Aires: La Nación, 1891), p. 248.

CHAPTER 3

THE PAMPA

The years of Jewish emigration to Argentina coincided with an era of profound change on the pampas. Not only was the Argentine population growing at an unprecedented rate, but the country had finally achieved a modicum of political stability under a capable and relatively liberal oligarchy of large landowners and cattle ranchers.

The country was becoming wealthy, and ostentatious signs of prosperity were everywhere. The pampa had been settled; the "barbaric" gaucho was marked for extinction, his passing mourned only by a few romantics. But the greatest changes occurred in Argentina's cities, especially Buenos Aires.

The capital city enjoyed a veneer of tranquility imparted by its control of beef and cereal exports, but underneath trouble was brewing. "New" immigrants, invariably linked in the minds of the elite with radical ideologies were, in the view of many increasingly nationalistic Argentine politicians and intellectuals, dissipating Argentina's promise rather than fulfilling it. For their part, newcomers busily organized to demand unheard-of changes in the political and social system.

The construction and expansion that characterized Buenos Aires around the turn of the century could not hide the fact that the lot of the working class remained a difficult one. The distribution of wealth and privilege was terribly inequitable. No one would have disputed Lord Bryce's remarks that "if the best parts of Buenos Aires are as tasteful as those of Paris there is plenty of ugliness in the worst suburbs."[1] Another observer noted that although Buenos Aires was "one of the most remarkable cities in the world, thousands whose hands and heads should be employed in making Argentina are crowding Buenos Aires to the verge of suffocation, struggling to earn a living, . . . starving in a country where starvation should be impossible, swelling the ranks of that human sediment. . . ."[2]

Most *porteños,* the inhabitants of Buenos Aires, did not benefit from the capital's modernization or from economic growth firmly rooted in agricultural exports. A small industrial sector, mostly devoted to food processing, did not produce enough to compete with imports from Europe or the United States. Argentina's need to import fuel and machinery to run its inefficient industries made the situation more difficult. An exporting country, Argentina was particularly sensitive to fluctuations in world market prices, especially those caused by shifts in European, and particularly British, demand. Argentina's own meat, grain, wool, and hides made up only a fraction of the world supply of these products, and commodity prices were fixed on world markets over which the country had little influence. As a result, export earnings rose and fell with distressing frequency; never, however did they plunge more alarmingly than during the Depression of 1890.[3]

The 1890 depression was the most serious crisis in Argentine economic history. Its shockwaves caused a rebellion against the government, the resignation of a president, the near collapse of an important British banking house, and a serious weakening of Argentina's position in international commerce. Domestically, the crisis increased unemployment in the laboring class, forcing many workers to emigrate. It drove down artificially inflated real estate values. It damaged the position of tradesmen in the capital, many of whom took to selling their inventories at public auction. The standard of living of the *porteño* working class remained depressed for more than a decade.[4]

In 1893 a British observer, describing the results of the crash, noted the consequences of Argentina's overreliance on primary products: "The poverty stricken appearance of the city [Buenos Aires] is in strange contrast to the lavish expenditure that characterized it three years ago. Unfinished buildings and public works are seen everywhere; the pavements of the streets are gradually breaking up, and scarcely any attempt is made to repair the damage. . . ."[5] The oligarchy's solution to the crisis was to seek still more foreign capital and implement austerity measures designed to restore Argentina's position as a good credit risk. But the underlying causes of the depression—the boom and bust economy that inevitably stemmed from reliance on agro-exports—remained unchanged.

The Argentine working class suffered most from these periodic economic crises. Even so unsympathetic a visitor as W. H. Koebel reluctantly confessed that "there is this, however, to be said for the complaints of some of the labouring class in Buenos Aires. It must be admitted that so far scarcely enough attention has been paid to the legitimate amusements of the humbler orders."[6] Class conflict, much of it centering on Buenos Aires, added to the worker's plight. Most found it difficult to achieve any meaningful upward social mobility. Although

Buenos Aires offered wages higher than those available in other cities, the cost of living was higher still.[7] While the monetary and fiscal policies of the Argentine government kept real wages depressed, the high cost of food, dwelling, and consumer goods from abroad ate deeply into workers' wages. *Porteños* paid for many goods not as Argentine consumers but as European consumers, a long and expensive distance from the original markets.

Argentina's commitment to free trade and restrictive monetary policies drove prices up leaving it to depressions to correct price imbalances. The net effect of the cycle was to limit employment—even during prosperous years more than five percent of the workforce was idle, while during economic crises unemployment reached 20 percent. Besides those counted in such statistics, Buenos Aires housed a permanent army of disguised unemployed, often self-employed traders and hawkers, who barely eked out livelihoods.

One early result of working class discontent was the founding of the Argentine Socialist party in 1896. Created and led by respected members of the middle class, the Socialists sought to secure a more just society through cooperativism and electoral participation. Until the passage of the Saenz Peña Electoral Reform Law in 1912, though, limited franchise made the Socialist platform a pipe dream. And after 1912, the party suffered from rampant electoral fraud and the lack of Socialist strength in the interior.[8] The Socialist party never posed a real threat to the Argentine system.

The Socialists appealed to skilled workers, whom they tried to educate in the ways of bourgeois civic responsibility. As Lord Bryce noted, "in the cities there exists, between the wealthy and the workingmen, a considerable body of professional men, shopkeepers, and clerks, who are rather less of a well-defined middle class than they would be in Europe."[9] The party also urged immigrants, who otherwise could not vote, to become Argentine citizens. But very few Jews, at least, chose to assume the burdens that accompanied naturalization. (Only some 24,500 of the estimated 360,000 Jews in Argentina had become naturalized by 1953).[10]

Although many Jews are presumed to have been partisans of the Socialist party, the relationship was sometimes an uneasy one. In particular, the position of Socialist elder stateman Juan B. Justo on assimilation made many Jews uncomfortable. In an article written for the Jewish magazine *Vida Nuestra* in 1923, Justo presented his feelings on what he believed was a valid distinction between Jews as a people and as individuals. Himself married to a Russian Jewish woman, Justo nevertheless wrote, "all together Jews immediately become enigmatic and suspicious to me." He also complained that Jewish tradition, so different from that of the Argentine majority, reflected "a spirit that will not contribute anything to national unity and energy." Moderately sympathetic to Zionism, Justo advised his readers to "abdicate, as Jews, from secret pride, and the word 'Jew' will more quickly lose its present offensive connotation."[11] Such sentiments did not endear him to those he addressed.

The same low wages, longer hours, and desperation that led Argentine workers to political action more radical than that offered by the Socialists also roused Jewish workers and the petty bourgeoisie. Trade unions and commercial associations were formed to help counter the vagaries of the Argentine economy. Although Jewish unions were not especially successful, the forces that led Jewish workers to organize do shed some light on the nature of working-class life in the Jewish community in Buenos Aires.

When the first Jewish workers arrived in Argentina from Russia, many sought work from their western European coreligionists. Others soon became employers. This occupational fluidity led one contemporary to note that these first workers "had no notion of class. The fact that, at its foundings in 1897, both bosses and workers belonged to the Jewish Worker's Center is proof of this."[12] However, there is more to this phenomenon than an apparent absence of class consciousness. The nature of workshop production—the fact that workers could become owners and then workers again—blurred distinctions between the two groups. Jewish workers, contractors, and owners had all experienced this form of mobility in Russia, and they brought it with them to the New World. As production modernized, class lines within the community rigidified and traditional distinctions between workers and owners asserted themselves.

The second wave of Jewish immigration, coinciding with the Kishineff pogrom and the Russian revolution in 1905, contributed to a heightened degree of militancy among Jewish workers. Many of these Jewish workers had already been exposed to a wide variety of socialist parties in Europe. In 1906, Jews established a Socialist-Zionist (Poalei Zion) party in the Argentine capital. Under aggressive leadership, the Poalei Zion achieved some degree of influence in the Jewish community. It focused mainly on the autocratic policies of the Jewish Colonization Association, which, while concerned with the management and administration of the colonies, affected urban Jews with relatives and friends in the colonies almost as much as it did the colonists themselves.

The party was dealt a severe blow in 1910, when many of its

leaders were deported during a period of heightened class tension and anti-immigrant feeling. But it again became something of a factor in the community after the announcement of the Balfour Declaration in 1917, when Britain recognized the right of the Jews to a homeland in Palestine.[13]

Because the majority of all Argentine workers found that the Socialist party did not address their real needs, the anarchists, who were more radical, rapidly became the most powerful faction in the fledgling Argentine labor movement. Their direct-action tactics, especially the general strike, made the anarchists a force to be reckoned with. Enough Jews joined the anarchist movement to prompt *La Protesta,* the movement's organ, to publish a page in Yiddish for fourteen months between 1908 and 1909. Although the anarchists' precarious financial position put an end to this regular service, the movement continued to publish occasional works in Yiddish.

In March 1908, a group of young working-class Jewish activists announced to the Argentine labor movement the formation of the Committee for Union Agitation. The Committee held that militants in the Argentine labor movement gave relatively little attention to Jewish workers because of the language barrier, and the committee proposed, in effect, to act as translators for organized labor. It also offered to teach Jewish workers about labor unions, to encourage their participation in them, and to establish a Jewish organizing committee composed of representatives from various existing unions.[14]

Jewish tailors, carpenters, bakers, and others all formed unions in the first decade of the century. Coordinating the efforts of these unions was never easy; the carpenters and tailors allied themselves with the Socialist trade union federation (the UGT), while the bakers joined the anarchist trade union federation (FORA). The Jewish tailors union formed in 1908, with help from the Committee for Union Agitation. Scarcity of work, however, led to the union's quick dissolution. Seasonal unions, strong when there was work and all but invisible during the slow season, were a fact of life for early needle-trades organizers.

Carpenters struck in 1908 and 1909 to abolish the piecework system, which at that time accounted for 90 percent of all furniture production. The strike did limit the summer work day to nine hours and the winter day to eight, but it was not successful in eliminating piecework. Furthermore, within a few years splits over ideology and tactics crippled the Jewish carpenters union.[15]

The horrible working conditions in the bakeries of Buenos Aires made these Jews among the city's most militant workers. Associated with the anarchists, bakers played an important role in many of Buenos

Aires' labor disputes. Bakeries were located in deep subcellars and had no access to fresh air. Primitive ovens generated intense heat. Bakers worked all night in conditions that contemporaries compared to stables. They slept on straw mats that did little to protect them from accumulated dampness. In an attempt to improve their lives, bakers struck for the first time in 1909. They demanded an eight-hour day, an end to overtime, adoption of the union label, the imposition of an indemnity on their employer, and funds to provide for the wife of a worker who fell ill during his detention for strike activities. But by 1912, bakers had won only the right to restrict work in Jewish-owned bakeries to Jewish workers.[16]

In 1907, a group of Jewish Bundists founded *Avanguard (Vanguard),* a periodical devoted to propagating socialism among Jews in general and those in the working class in particular. *Avanguard* opposed anti-immigrant legislation, supported the formation of Jewish trade unions, and endorsed the minimum program of the Argentine Socialist party.

Questions of culture and nationalism almost always plagued the Jewish left. Shortly after its founding, *Avanguard* split between those who favored autonomy and those who supported links with the Socialists. The Bundists had struggled with the question of language in Russia and had, as a result, become fervent advocates of Yiddish, the language of the Jewish masses. Yiddish had been given new respectability when Jewish intellectuals in Russia and the United States developed a culture based on its use. Speaking in Yiddish became an article of faith among Bundists all over the world, including Argentina.[17] They sought to have the language used in newspapers, magazines, libraries, schools, and cultural programs. The Socialists, meanwhile, tolerated Yiddish but only as an organizing tool until workers could be taught Spanish.

THE 1910 REPRESSION

Cultural questions, but ones posed by Argentine intellectuals, played a prominant role in the first widespread organized attack on the Jewish community of Buenos Aires. As the country approached its centennial celebration in 1910, intensifying labor agitation, linked by hostile intellectuals and politicians to the presence of immigrants, set off the so-called "nationalist restoration." Voices throughout the country complained that immigrant schools educated children in alien traditions.[18] Both *La Nación* and *La Prensa,* Buenos Aires' leading daily newspapers, vigorously attacked immigrant schools and demanded Argentine educations for all.

The real question in the debate was the political function of education. For the nationalists, the correct role of the school was to teach respect for Argentina's past and instill pride in its future greatness. Immigrants, on the other hand, saw education as a means to preserve their traditional culture. Although other immigrant communities were mentioned, the harshest attacks were reserved for Jewish schools. By 1910, anti-immigrant feelings, especially anti-Jewish sentiment, was at fever pitch.

At regular intervals between 1900 and 1910, anarchists led general strikes in Buenos Aires. Violence was not uncommon as workers and police confronted each other in the streets. The most serious encounter took place on May 1, 1909, when cavalry, under the command of Colonel Ramón Falcón, charged a protest march and left more than eighty wounded and fourteen dead; no police were hurt.[19] Six months later, Simon Radowitzky, a young Russian Jewish anarchist, retaliated by assassinating Falcón.[20] Anti-immigrant feelings heightened. In May 1910, while Congress considered imposing a state of siege, mobs destroyed the offices of *La Protesta* and *La Vanguardia,* the anarchist and Socialist dailies. Unruly crowds fell upon Russian Jewish neighborhoods and left a trail of destruction in their wake. The Russian Library, the most important working class cultural center in the Jewish community, was sacked. A few days later, Argentina's centennial festivities, in which the "other" Argentina showed its best face to the world, did take place, but the atmosphere was still highly charged.

Unrest in the working class provoked both cooptation and repression in the years to come. Successive governments attempted to stifle the labor movement and succeeded in severely weakening it. Congress enacted legislation that authorized the government to forbid entry to any immigrant suspected of radical political activity and to deport more easily those it considered dangerous agitators. Although the Saenz Peña law permitted previously excluded groups to participate in the formal political process, the indifference of immigrants to electoral politics limited the reform's impact. In fact, the willingness of Argentina's leaders to smother any opposition prevented any serious challenge to the assumptions that underlay Argentine politics and policies.

At least until 1916, *estancieros* (owners of large cattle ranches) ruled Argentina in a near vacuum. This oligarchy derived important support from *criollo* (native Argentine) "middle-class" interests. Over the years, though, many of these middle-class Argentines gravitated into the orbit of the Unión Civica Radical (UCR) or Radical Civic Union, a party the native Argentine middle class favored for its xenophobic condescension toward immigrants. The oligarchy also valued the UCR for its support of the Argentine system. The UCR, they understood, wanted a larger share of the pie for its members without changing the basic recipe.

In spite of Argentina's great wealth (in 1914 J. A. Hobson placed it among the five wealthiest nations in the world), Argentina faced an uncertain future as the shadows of war began to gather over Europe. The structural problems that the country failed to confront between 1880 and 1914 remained.[21] Argentine economic growth had for years been determined by its hegemonic agro-export sector, and the country's infrastructure, largely British-owned, had been designed to expedite the export of beef and grains. Economic well-being still depended on the variable success of agriculture because tradition, indifference, lack of investment capital, and a shortage of skilled labor combined to limit industrial expansion.

The six years that preceded World War I graphically illustrate the nature of Argentina's boom-and-bust economy. In 1908 demand for Argentina's raw materials slumped, and the economy suffered accordingly. But by 1913 the country had rebounded to enjoy a few years of prosperity. Exports rose in value, foreign capital continued to enter the republic, and a record harvest stuffed the holds of outgoing freighters. The next year, however, crop failures resulted in a flight of gold from the country, an end to capital investment, a decline in land values, the contraction of imports, and numerous commercial failures. By August 1914 recession had turned to depression and panic.

On the political front, the very few still controlled the workings of Buenos Aires and, for that matter, Argentina. Immigrants lived in harsh, unpleasant surroundings and optimistic official pronouncements notwithstanding, faced a difficult future. The continued backing by the UCR of the export sector's dominance, and a social structure dominated by *estancieros,* did little to improve matters. Subtle political changes, however, were taking place in the years before World War I. The Radicals, or members of the UCR, were more aware of the urban immigrant than the oligarchy had been, and the party sought the support of immigrants. In preparation for the 1916 campaign, the Radical machine organized and propagandized in immigrant barrios. Handbills, printed in Yiddish, circulated through Jewish neighborhoods.[22] In the final analysis though, it was the Saenz Peña law that guaranteed the election of the UCR's leader, Hipólito Irigoyen, to the presidency in 1916, Irigoyen's victory belonged to the native Argentine middle class, because most immigrants did not vote.

The conditions that Irigoyen faced in 1916 were inauspicious. Despite its wartime neutrality, Argentina entered yet another economic downturn. Unemployment stood at 16 percent and the cost of living continued to rise.[23] To this worsening situation President Irigoyen brought an ill-defined program that favored rural Argentina and strived for the opportunistic mediation of labor disputes, with resort to outright repression when necessary.

By November 1916, the situation had deteriorated to the point where the government converted the Immigrant Hotel into a hostel for the unemployed. For the first time, too, requests for support, loans, and subsidies from Jews in Buenos Aires and the colonies began to figure prominently in the records of the Chevrah Keduscha and other Jewish voluntary associations. Although some requests appeared to be extraordinary ones—25 pesos to aid Jewish war victims in Palestine or a loan of 70 pesos to permit one member of the Chevrah to enroll his two orphaned granddaughters in high school—others indicate that daily problems confronted the community. For example, the Chevrah alloted 100 pesos to the colonists of Porvenir to ease their financial burden.

Gradually the Chevrah expanded its attempts to counter poverty. On May 17, 1915, the Chevrah proposed issuing poverty cards that would allow members to defray dues for three months at a time until they were able to pay. In late November, the Chevrah gave 30 pesos to ease the distress of four babies whose father had died and whose mother was hospitalized. (The case was referred to the Sociedad Ezrah, which dealt directly with the community's health matters). Indeed, the problem of orphans and widows became so severe that in December the executive committee of the Chevrah unanimously voted to establish a fund for them, although it defeated a motion to increase dues to raise the needed money. On the eve of Passover 1916, it budgeted 200 pesos for the distribution of matzoh (traditional unleavened bread eaten to commemorate the exodus from Egypt) to the poor. In addition to such outright grants and loans, the Chevrah also tried to create jobs for people. Thus it alloted 15 pesos to "provide a poor man with a cigarette stand."[24]

World War I brought with it severe unemployment, limiting the opportunities for working-class organization and driving many workers completely out of the country. The recession caused Jewish capmakers to suspend their union activities after only one year of operation. Economic problems were exacerbated by the competition between Socialists and anarchists for the loyalty of the working class. The result was that in 1917 Jewish carpenters founded an independent organization free from sectarian splits. Tailors and bakers pursued a similar course. In the next several years anti-immigrant legislation, wartime layoffs, further repression, and theoretical and sectarian splits weakened the Jewish labor movement beyond repair.[25] As a separate but affiliated entity, it did not survive past 1920.

Data indicate that almost 700,000 people left Argentina between 1914 and 1919.[26] These emigrants were not *golondrinas,* the mostly Italian and Spanish agricultural workers who crossed the ocean to work in the harvests and then returned to Europe; they were people who had intended to settle in Argentina. Unemployment and the high cost of living for the working class drove them elsewhere.[27]

For those who stayed, making ends meet was difficult. The war meant that staple foods "in many instances are subject to daily fluctuations according to the stocks on hand, which . . . were very low owing to the infrequent arrivals of cargo vessels from abroad." Also, " . . . there has been a very considerable advance in all prices in question, which has compelled the poorer part of the population to cease purchasing some of these articles that were previously common in every home."[28] The high cost of living would plague *porteños* throughout Irigoyen's administration.

Charity from voluntary associations, or the earnings of wives and children, often meant the difference between remaining in Argentina and emigrating or between having a home and being evicted. In the decade between 1914 and 1924 there occurred a striking increase in the employment of minors; the relationship between dwindling real earnings and the number of children employed is all too clear.[29] Homework, piecework, and child labor were all parts of trying to *"hacer la América"* (succeed in America).

THE TRAGIC WEEK

The militancy of the Argentine working class, the success of the Russian Revolution, and Communist movements in Hungary and Germany contributed to an atmosphere in which talk of revolution circulated freely in Buenos Aires. In December 1918, metalworkers struck the firm of Pedro Vasena and Sons, Ltd. In spite of the heavy-handedness of the police, the workers remained on strike, and tensions ran high as the year ended. Amid intensified violence, the anarchists called a general strike for January 8, 1919. On the appointed day, the streets of Buenos Aires were empty. In the week that followed, the situation escalated into a full-blown confrontation between labor and capital. Class hostility offered the prospect of civil war.

By January 10, groups of armed civilians united against the working class were accompanying police on their rounds. The Irigoyen government, recovered from its initial paralysis, called on patriotic Argentines to defend the country from the cadres of "Maximalist" (bolshevik) foreigners, adding nativist and anti-Semitic dimensions to what had been a class struggle.

Armed mobs roamed the streets in search of *Rusos* (Russians, by this time synonymous with Jews) and other immigrant groups. On the night of the 10th, vigilantes and police sacked the headquarters of *Avanguard* and of Poalei Zion, destroying their furniture and libraries. They also attacked the offices of the Jewish bakers and furworkers unions. Jews living in the center of Buenos Aires, and in the barrios of Once, Villa Crespo, Caballito, and La Boca-Barracas, were terrorized.[30]

Just as tempers showed signs of cooling, the police announced the discovery of a "Communist" plot to take over Argentina. They arrested Pedro Wald, a Yiddish journalist with socialist leanings, and accused him of being the Argentine Lenin. When Wald and his alleged coconspirators were released a week later, it became obvious that the charges were baseless.

On January 13, Admiral Domecq Garcia, with the support of Argentine and foreign capital, formed a civil guard to defend the regime. Russian Jews amounted to more than half of the 2,000 people arrested that day. The following day, after a week in which 700 people died, 4,000 were injured, and thousands more were arrested and deported, the city returned to work.[31]

The gross statistics obscure the suffering and degradation that the Jewish community experienced during *Semana Trágica* (Tragic Week). Juan José de Soiza Reilly, an Argentine journalist, reported "the martyrdom of the innocents," describing "old men whose beards were torn out . . . ," one whose ribs "protruded from his skin like needles, bleeding . . . ," a woman "forced to eat her own excrement. . . ," and "teenage girls who had been raped by marauding bands."[32] José Mendelsohn, a prominent Jewish intellectual and historian of the community, wrote that Russian pogroms "were child's play compared to what happened . . . . cavalrymen dragged old Jews through the streets of Buenos Aires naked, throwing them by their grey beards, their skin torn and scraped against the cobblestones, while the sabres and whips of the men on horseback struck intermittently on their bodies."[33]

The hastily formed Committee of the Community prepared a partial list of people who had been killed or injured during the pogrom. All but four were workers. Samuel Muller, whose widow received some money from the Chevrah, was shot to death by a policeman while trying to get out of harm's way. According to an eyewitness, the murderer, one Cattaneo, yelled, "so we will kill all of your countrymen." Muller, a tailor liked and respected by his neighbors, was survived by his widow, aged twenty-nine, and three daughters, aged five, four, and one. Bernardo Razumney, a twenty-five year-old glazier, and a companion were luckier. Arrested on the morning of the 13th, they were taken to the ninth precinct, where they were soon freed through the intervention of a friendly auxiliary policeman. At noon the same day, several soldiers and civilians detained the two men in their homes and took from them two glazier's diamonds. In one of numerous cases of theft, the police never mentioned the gems again. Picked up a second time that day, the two men were taken to police headquarters, where they were beaten. Razumney, who joined the Chevrah in 1920, was a widower with a two-year-old child and had been in Argentina since 1912.[34]

As did many rightists, both Argentine and foreign, U. S. Ambassador to Argentina F. J. Stimson believed that bolsheviks masterminded the general strike. The embassy received early casualty figures indicating that most of the dead and wounded were Jews. Stimson also recalled meeting a military man who told him that 179 of the 193 workers whose bodies had been identified were Russian Jews.[35]

Anti-Semitism had been building in the upper and middle classes long before the Tragic Week erupted. For years, Argentine students had been exposed to textbooks teaching, among other things, that the Jews "monopolized the sustenance of other peoples," and that "in Russia lived 6,000,000 Jews, all of them innkeepers, usurers, and owners of holes in the wall [small shops]." The Baron Hirsch was described as "bringing expelled Jews to Argentina to create [here] a new Palestine."[36] Many had read Julian Martel's bestselling novel of 1891, *La Bolsa,* serialized in *La Nación,* which blamed the country's financial woes on Jewish financiers. The Catholic church, too, contributed to anti-Semitic agitation. Engaged in a fierce struggle with the radicals for the loyalties of the working class, priests on streetcorners railed against anarchists and Jews. Even in Jewish neighborhoods, clerics like Monsignor Napal attacked Jews as traitors and socialists, blaming them for wartime shortages.[37]

Of course, avarice merged with anti-Semitism during the Tragic Week. The Committee of the Community cited several instances in which police and civilian auxiliaries robbed Jews. Soiza Reilly reported that some grocers thought that they could reduce competition by killing Jews. Still, the oligarchy's injection of anti-Semitic beliefs "to deaden the minds of the people and introduce chaos and panic into the politics of the country, . . . to excite and confuse . . . the honest and legal struggle against the action or inaction of the government . . ." was a powerful force behind the violence that occurred.[38]

One effect of the tragedy was to shatter the prevailing myth of a classless society, making politics in Argentina more polarized than before. Through such organizations as the Argentine Patriotic League, the oligarchy exerted constant pressure on the politically vulnerable Irigoyen and narrowed his options in negotiating with organized labor. It became obvious that no subsequent administration could make real overtures to workers or intervene effectively on their behalf until the power of the oligarchy and its European supporters was curbed. The Tragic Week showed that Argentina's elite, allied with foreign capital, were still better prepared to suppress a revolution than the working class was to make one.

The Tragic Week, Argentina's first full-scale pogrom, also changed the Jewish community in several ways. Leaders more fully perceived the community's precarious position (indeed, the Chevrah gave 1,000 pesos to support "a competent defense"). Prominent Jewish voluntary associations and institutions, as well as the Socialist deputation in Congress, vigorously defended the Jews' patriotism, diligence, and contributions to Argentine life. In speeches, newspapers, magazine articles, wall posters, and the statements of the Committee of the Community, Jews and their supporters protested the excesses of the mob and demanded indemnities. The Argentine Zionist Federation (FSA), in conjunction with other community groups, issued a moderate statement that separated the hardworking majority of Jews from a "hotheaded minority."[39]

The willingness of the conservative and relatively successful Jewish leadership to accept the validity of many reactionary allegations against Jews further split the community along class lines. For instance, rather than defending all Jews against anti-Semitic outrages, the FSA acted in such a way as to isolate a militant minority of the community, obviously workers. Similarly, the Congregación Israelita, the synagogue usually associated with the well-to-do, joined many other organizations in announcing to non-Jewish Argentines that "150,000 honest men of all stations, from all classes, affiliated with all political parties, speak to you through us, to prevent an inexplicable crime. . . . Let the justice that you are preparing for the offenders, whom we repudiate, be inexorable and severe, but let it correspond to the faith we have in you. Don't persecute the innocent." Meanwhile, working-class organizations pulled fewer punches. One leader of the Poalei Zion wrote that "once more Jews pay for the crime of being Jews," while the Bund argued that the bolshevik threat "was an excuse to attack the labor movement, in general, and the Jewish population, in particular."[40] Overall, the Jewish community split along the same general lines that marked all of Argentine politics.

The effects of the public relations campaign undertaken by the leaders of the Jewish community are difficult to determine, but the leadership apparently realized that more was needed to protect Jews from anti-Semitic Argentines. In April, prominent Jews secured an interview with President Irigoyen. As described by the Executive Committee of the Chevrah: "[We] were cordially received by the president. Once [we] expounded on the rumors circulating about, which grieve the entire Jewish colony, he replied favorably and promised that there is no reason for the community to be upset. He intended to meet with the Chief of Police on the same subject to take the necessary measures."[41]

The Jewish community's leaders had learned well the rules of politics as defined by the Radical party. The president, enjoying his role as protector of the oppressed, was the final arbiter. But coordination among immigrant leaders, most of them entrepreneurs, was limited, because such men had few contacts with the political elite and the Radical party. "This failure of communication occurred because the system of selection of the political elite discriminated against the immigrants, who prompted the great majority of industrial undertakings."[42]

The hegemony of the oligarchy was so complete that no other bourgeois theory of development, such as was being embodied by many immigrant entrepreneurs, had a chance to take root. This hegemony was not threatened by appeals from certain kinds of immigrants; namely, those who had become economically successful and by their example justified the oligarchy's support of Argentine immigration policy. The Jewish community leadership's appeal to Irigoyen reflected assumptions that they shared with him. Each understood power in the same way and recognized that the appeal for protection was not a threat to the beliefs they held in common.

The existence of such channels of redress throws the question of immigrant participation in politics into a new light. A chain of communication that allowed the leaders of voluntary associations to seek Irigoyen's personal intervention may have given aliens a sense of political participation even if they could not vote. The result was a facade of flexibility; the system appeared less rigidly controlled than in fact it was.[43]

In 1921, the Argentine government tightened its immigration policies to help combat growing unemployment. A minimum requirement, often impossible for immigrants from war-torn countries to fulfill, was complete documentation. Eastern European Jews found it difficult to obtain visas. Argentine consuls in Europe, responsible for weeding out undesirables, became increasingly cautious. Argentina's preference for skilled industrial workers or experienced farmers further restricted immigration. These biases, though not anti-Semitic in origin, had the effect of hindering Jewish immigration.

In October, community leaders sought Irigoyen's intervention again to ease the restrictions on Jewish immigration, and in 1922 the Jewish Colonization Association received a guarantee (withdrawn the following year) of preferential treatment for Jewish immigrants. Perhaps in return for services rendered, the Executive Committee of the Chevrah approved a donation of 300 pesos to a committee honoring Irigoyen when the president left office in 1922. A similar tribute was rendered upon Irigoyen's re-election in 1928.[44]

Although some Jews continued to join the Radical party, the Tragic Week temporarily embittered most Jews against Irigoyen and his party. *El Diario,* for example, reported that several Jewish Radicals resigned from the party when leaders from the Buenos Aires branch boasted of their role in massacring forty-eight Jews during one day of the strike.[45]

In the aftermath of the Tragic Week, some Jews registered their dissatisfaction with the community's leadership by forming the Partido Israelita Argentina (Jewish Argentine Party, PIA) to "organize citizens of Jewish origin on the social and political level to defend the future security of the Jews and support its millenarian culture for the good of the country. . . ."[46] The PIA actively backed candidates of the Socialist and Progressive Democrat parties in congressional elections. It advocated easing the naturalization laws, which effectively limited the possibility of electoral success for immigrants. The PIA also favored legalized divorce, abolition of anti-Semitic school books, and social legislation to protect workers. Campaigning in Yiddish and in Spanish, the PIA railed against Irigoyen's Radicals, accusing some of them of "satiating their perverse instincts on the defenseless members of the Jewish community. . . ."[47]

Whether the Partido Israelita Argentina could have become a viable entity in a country where class-based rather than ethnic politics predominated, is doubtful. Jews comprised only a small percentage of

Argentina's total population, even within Buenos Aires. Moreover, the potential effectiveness of an explicitly Jewish working-class party was further limited by the narrowness of its support. Only those active in the Bund or in Poalei Zion could favor at the same time a Jewish political party and non-Jewish candidates who made explicit appeals to the Jewish community; most Jews, including the Jewish press, did not simply assess candidates based on their stances regarding issues of importance to Jews. Nevertheless, the idea of a Jewish political party represented an innovative response to anti-Semitic and antiworking-class policies.

Nothing so graphically illustrates the plurality of viewpoints within the Jewish community as the existence of the Pro-Argentine Jewish League. Formed by a handful of wealthy Jews with no ties to the community, this group joined the Argentine Patriotic League, an organization that evolved from the White Guard, which terrorized the Jewish barrios during the Tragic Week.

The increasing fractionation of policies not only within the Jewish community but within all of Argentina shaped many of the government's decisions during the period. For instance, in 1921, the municipal council of Buenos Aires authorized the construction of a Jewish cemetery in the city. However, in 1925 the aristocratic Sociedad de Beneficencia (Beneficent Society), which had in the meantime purchased the adjacent property, asked the council to reverse itself and deny the community its cemetery. After years of wrangling and debate, during which the Radicals supported the Chevrah and the Socialists opposed it, the Chevrah was denied its land. It sold the property and opened its second cemetery away from the city, in Buenos Aires province. Perhaps as a result of the acrimony generated, and out of a desire to avoid any hint of anti-Semitism, the council proceeded to bar the establishment of new burial grounds within the city's limits.[48]

THE JEWISH COMMUNITY UNDER THE RADICALS

The records of the Chevrah Keduscha indicate that Irigoyen's administration did little to improve the economic and social well-being of the Jewish community of Buenos Aires. By the end of World War I, the Chevrah had substantial experience in dealing with poverty and provided several types of assistance. Although the Chevrah had no jobs itself to offer, in many instances it helped people to provide for themselves. Thus a widow with six small children received 245 pesos so that she could open a small business. In April 1922, another widow received some old fabrics and 100 pesos to purchase a sewing machine so that she could become a pieceworker. When the Chevrah gave 20 pesos to a man to open a cigarette stand so that he might support himself and his wife, it also wrote a letter to the man's son rebuking him for not contributing to his parents' support. Occasionally, too, the Chevrah intervened to improve someone's chances of gaining work. It agreed to send the three children of a widower to a shelter so that the man would be free to find a job. In addition, the Chevrah continued its tradition of supporting other voluntary associations by giving the Sociedad Ezrah, for instance, 100 pesos to help subsidize the distribution of clothes and shoes to the poor on the 9th of July, an Argentine holiday. In one instance, the Chevrah also gave rent money to a woman in danger of being evicted from her apartment because her husband had been in jail for three months. Illness and disability— cancer, tuberculosis, heart disease, amputation—also prompted the Chevrah to provide assistance, such as when it gave 100 pesos to one family so that the husband could stay home to care for his cancer-stricken wife.

The association also considered a wide variety of special requests, solicitations that provide insight into other concerns of the community. It was asked, for example, to contribute 5,000 pesos to a fund for the widow of Yiddish poet I. L. Peretz. It paid for the first Passover seder of the Jewish Popular Kitchen in 1923, gave the Palestine Workers' Fund 350 pesos for a seeding machine, and allotted 200 pesos to ease the burdens of "Jewish immigrants arriving here, abandoned, by the hundreds." For all its largesse, however, the Chevrah could not avoid the anger of at least one of its beneficiaries. On December 22, 1918, the executive committee was told by its president that a widow had returned the 75 pesos she had been given because "she thought she would be given a sum three or four times that. She refused to be humiliated by seeing her name listed in the Jewish press with those of other widows for such an insignificant sum." The president continued, "she refuses the donation on the advice of relatives who have promised to ease her economic situation."[49]

Even though the lives of Jews in Buenos Aires improved little, if any, during Irigoyen's first administration, it remains a watershed in Argentine history, despite falling short of the promise it offered in 1916. Although he never tackled the problem of land reform, Argentina's most pressing political issue, Irigoyen did expand the role of the state in the economy. He also used his authority, however inconsistently, to settle labor disputes, sought to limit the influence of British capital in railroads, and oversaw the creation of the Yacimientos Petrolíferos Fiscales (YPF), the state petroleum monopoly. Still, he did not use his power to improve the lot of the working class, and his cynical treatment of such issues as the high cost of living and tariff protection was always motivated by partisan political considerations. The administration's record in social welfare and labor legislation lagged behind those of Argentina's neighbors, Chile and Uruguay, but its record in education and public health was more respectable. In 1922, Argentines were better educated and lived longer than people in neighboring countries.[50]

A modest amount of industrialization did take place under Irigoyen. Argentina's wartime neutrality and the interruption of normal trading patterns with Europe—the number of ships clearing the port of Buenos Aires fell some 85 percent during the war—resulted in a forced and short-lived industrialization program to replace imports.[51] Nevertheless, in 1920 the U.S. Department of Commerce concluded that "manufacturing has only made a beginning there. Coal has not yet been discovered, and the centers of population and industry are removed from available water power. Rich in agricultural wealth, Argentina will remain for many years to come primarily an agricultural country."[52] Only those industries that processed food were well developed. The others, in the words of the Commerce Department "[were] comparatively trifling and [were] quite insufficient to meet local demands. A study of Argentina's trade clearly reveals . . . the general economic position of the country as an exporter of foodstuffs and an importer of many types of manufactured articles, such as clothing, machinery, railroad equipment and hundreds of other items of manufactured goods."[53]

In those industries in which tariff protection was effective, shoes and wearing apparel for example, some progress took place. In other cases, there was not enough protection to promote growth. Commodities essential for industrial expansion, especially fuel, remained in chronically short supply; Irigoyen's petroleum monopoly had more political impact than economic influence.

In spite of the many disappointments that surrounded his term of office, Irigoyen succeeded in making Radicalism the most potent force in Argentine politics, and in 1922 he easily handed power over to his chosen successor, Marcelo T. de Alvear. Scion of the aristocracy, long-time resident of Paris, and a member of the UCR's conservative wing, Alvear eventually came to preside over an anti-Irigoyen movement (antipersonalism, as the Argentines called it) that split the party.

Alvear's six years in the presidency were marked by a sound

existence for most. Argentines were calm and enjoyed "stable currency, full employment and abundant housing." According to Argentine historian Féliz Luna, "the Alvear administration was characterized by almost unprecedented prosperity. The value of land
increased at an astronomical rate, and wages went up much faster than
prices, thus giving the middle and lower classes perhaps the most
comfortable standard of living they had yet enjoyed."[54]

New municipal initiatives helped reduce the cost of living in
Buenos Aires in the first full year of Alvear's presidency. On January
8, 1923, for example, the Intendancy sought to lower prices on consumer goods by replacing middlemen. It empowered the Board of Supply and Price Reduction of Consumer Goods to open booths in city
markets, in public fairs, and on private premises to sell goods directly
to *porteños*.[55]

Employment in Buenos Aires increased substantially between
February 1923 and August 1924 and more slowly through February
1926.[56] But not all was well—the agricultural laboring population and
the acreage under cultivation were both declining. Between 1914 and
1924, Argentina gained an average of only about 10,000 immigrants a
year, many of whom settled in cities. Rural in-migration further exacerbated the country's demographic imbalance and caused the government to fear a permanent decline in agricultural output. It offered
newcomers and the unemployed jobs in the interior, but few listened.

Moreover, Alvear was not immune from the boom-and-bust economy that tormented his predecessors. Although during 1924 a general
improvement in the world business conditions stimulated overseas demand for Argentine exports, this affluence was fleeting. Fiscal 1924–
1925 and 1925 and 1926 were depression years. Crops fell short of
expectations and cereal prices plummeted. To compensate, the administration reduced imports and indulged in extensive borrowing, mainly
from New York banks. Temporarily, the bailout worked, because the
1926–1927 harvest was excellent and the following years exports ex-
ceeded one billion dollars for the first time since 1920. Increased gold
imports after 1926 provided the basis for greater purchasing power and
heightened commercial activity. But the end of Alvear's term coincided, more or less, with the constriction of the U.S. money market
that presaged the Great Depression. Borrowing and direct U. S. investment declined temporarily, exacerbating Argentina's problems with its
currency and balance of payments.[57]

In aggregate terms, four of the six years between 1922 and 1928
were prosperous. But while employment increased and the cost of
living remained more stable than it had been under Irigoyen, the aver-

age Argentine working-class family still managed only to make ends meet. Between 1923 and 1924, average family income declined by 500 pesos. Of 1,000 families surveyed by government statisticians, 77.6 percent reported balanced budgets, 16.2 percent registered a surplus, and 6.2 percent operated at a deficit.[58] Income declined in 1926 but rose to the 1924 level in the last year of Alvear's administration.[59]

The ephemeral prosperity of the mid-1920s had even less impact on the poor in the Jewish community. The records of the Chevrah show a continuous stream of applications for assistance. Between September 1923 and January 1927, seventy-five people approached the Chevrah asking for work, but it had none to offer them. Others asked for and received help in setting up small businesses, especially selling cigarettes at kiosks or sewing. During the same period, almost 1,600 people received some form of general aid or subsidized loans. One applicant was refused permission to sell cigarettes in the Chevrah's lobby, but the association did offer to place two sisters in domestic service. Similarly, the executive committee chose to lend a camera to an applicant rather than give him the funds to buy one so that "he will have more need to work."

For the first time, several requests for funds to leave Buenos Aires or emigrate from Argentina appear in the Chevrah's records. One case involved a young woman, recently arrived from Russia, "who was brought to the country by her husband so that he might live off her." Rabbis had granted her a divorce, but she needed money for passage back to Russia. More than a dozen others petitioned for grants to leave Buenos Aires and go to the provinces, Uruguay, Russia, and the United States. Several others left the city on their own before the Chevrah had a chance to act on their cases.[60]

In 1927, thirty-nine people asked the executive committee to finance their exit from Buenos Aires. Interestingly, while six hundred applied for loans, subsidies, or general assistance, only nine asked the Chevrah to employ them. Perhaps the inability of the association to ease the unemployment crisis had become obvious. The following year, twenty people asked the Chevrah for work, forty-four asked for money to leave Buenos Aires, and five hundred and eighty sought some form of charity.[61]

In spite of the split within the Radical party, and the oligarchy's intensified hostility to his demogogy, the septuagenarian Irigoyen easily won re-election to the presidency in 1928. Under the by-then senile politician, the worst aspects of the Radical government—corruption, partisan excess, and the inability to act forcefully in an emergency— reappeared. As world market prices for primary products fell during the 1929 depression, Argentina's economic position deteriorated badly. The decline in purchasing power especially crushed wholesalers, importers, and domestic manufacturers.[62]

Prosperity extended into the first half of 1929 because of the previous year's harvest, but the second half of the year was worse than any similar period in the country's recent past. In 1930, domestic difficulties, underproduction, and currency depreciation coalesced to form a severe political and economic crisis.

THE FALL OF THE RADICALS

In March 1930 the Radical party suffered its first defeat in more than a decade in a Buenos Aires election. Six months later, on September 6, with the support of the oligarchy, the army overthrew the government—in part to clean up civilian politics. Thus began the infamous epoch Argentines remember as the decade in which military regimes and the civilian administrations that followed them returned the *estancieros* to overt political control.

The public initially seemed apathetic to the coup, but only temporarily. The Radicals won the 1931 election; the military annulled it. To remain in power, the generals and their conservative allies had to resort to the very policies for which they despised the Radicals. Political corruption and fraudulent elections became the order of the day. The military presence in politics became more important than ever, and Argentine nationalists achieved a far greater degree of influence than they had previously enjoyed.[63]

The 1930 Revolution brought General José F. Uriburu to power. Uriburu, motivated by a sense of economic nationalism absent in earlier administrations, encouraged domestic manufacture by creating national regulatory boards. The Exchange Control Commission (to regulate imports) and the National Commission for Industrial Development (to stimulate new industries) reflected the military's commitment to industralization. Uriburu also instituted a policy of moderate tariff protection. In February 1931, the regime raised tariffs on textiles, yarns, leather and leather goods, hats and caps, and several other products. The new president continued Alvear's policy of encouraging foreign investment, and a number of European and North American corporations opened Argentine subsidiaries.[64] However, aspiring industrialists, still dissatisfied, wanted more protection and political power.

Manufacturers were not the only discontented Argentines. The high cost of living, particularly in staple foods, continued to plague the residents of Buenos Aires. The Supply Board appealed to food dealers and landowners to reduce prices voluntarily. When those efforts failed, the municipality bought flour, bread, wheat, milk, meat, and vegetables to sell directly, at reduced prices, to the public.[65]

In 1931, the Depression's effect on internal purchasing power became increasingly noticeable. The buying power of the peso depreciated rapidly. Wages declined 17 percent between 1927 and 1931, while food and rent increased 7 and 5 percent, respectively.

Unemployment became and remained a serious problem. The British Board of Overseas Trade commented, "there is a good deal of privation and suffering, and this has been more noticeable during the winter months of 1930 than at previous periods."[66] In 1932, a census of the unemployed counted almost 140,000 men permanently unemployed before January 1, 1931, and another 110,000 subsequently idled. About 70,000 others were either seasonally or partially unemployed.[67]

Throughout the Depression, the Chevrah Keduscha continued to treat poverty on an individual basis through jobs, loans, and subsidies. It also expanded its operations to fund institutions created to ease the burden of the poor. The executive committee tried "to deal with the matter of raising funds for lodging for the many unemployed so they will not have to sleep in the public plazas." One suggestion involved purchasing a house for the Cocina Popular Israelita (Jewish Popular Kitchen). The proposed building was to be located in the barrio of Villa Crespo "where the greatest number of needy and poor are to be found. This will allow them to save the cost of the tramway when they go to eat."[68]

As if the burden on the Chevrah were already not heavy enough, sample data reveal that more than 13 percent of the 1925 sample dropped out of the Chevrah, three quarters of them between 1930 and 1940. Between 1930 and 1940, slightly less than 20 percent of the 1930 sample stopped paying membership dues. That more than half of this group did not resume paying dues until after 1940 suggests that economic recovery was a long time in coming to the Jewish community.[69]

Uriburu's power steadily declined, and in November 1931, he was replaced by General Augustín P. Justo, a man with great ambition but more limited political goals. Justo ruled until 1938, his term characterized by a national recovery program, currency reform, continued electoral fraud, and the negotiation of the Roca-Runciman pacts with Great Britain. These treaties reduced the cost of British exports, making them more competitive on the Argentine market. Justo also agreed to the benevolent treatment of British capital and granted English firms the monopoly on the public transportation system in Buenos Aires. In return, the British promised to continue to purchase Argentine beef.

Despite these efforts, the economy continued its downturn. Between 1930 and 1934, market prices for Argentina's major exports—meat, wheat, hides, and wool—fell 40 percent, a drop that cost the primary sector $600 million a year.[70] Although the number of bankruptcies reported declined somewhat, the improvement was the result only of reduced commercial activity. Almost 30 percent of these bankruptcies were private failures with a value that increased from 65.9 million pesos in 1930 to 88.1 million pesos in 1934. Failures among farmers and livestock breeders increased almost 350 percent and drove provincials, among them many inhabitants of the original Jewish Colonization Association colonies, to large cities. Certain sectors of the economy, such as textiles, did register some gains. Factory bankruptcies fell from 8 million to 260,000 pesos, importers' from almost 13 million to 7.7 million pesos, and retail stores' from 24 million to 13.3 million pesos.[71]

Although recovery began in 1935, the cost of living continued to rise, and food prices, up 15.3 percent between 1935 and 1936, contributed substantially to the increase. Friendly to foreign capital and the agro-export sector, the Justo administration governed for their benefit, with results that proved costly to the working class. For example, the Roca-Runciman pacts, renewed in 1936, extended Argentina's unpopular ties with England.[72]

Civilian opposition to these policies grew. In 1938, Justo allowed a presidential election, but rather than risking a return to the abhorrent policies of the Radicals, the administration stole votes and announced the election of Roberto Ortiz. Ortiz attempted to democratize the system, but in 1940, crippled by diabetes, he resigned in favor of his vice president, Ramón Castillo. The new president continued Argentina's policy of neutrality, which, as during World War I, resulted in wartime industrialization programs to make up for lost imports. This added to the industrialization that had finally begun in earnest in Argentina during the 1930s. Expansion took place largely in the manufacture of consumer goods and food processing, and, for the first time, Argentina made extensive use of domestic raw materials. In 1943, also for the first time, the value of industrial production surpassed that of agriculture.

The Second World War caused severe dislocations among Argentine workers, and in 1940 the country had some 180,000 unemployed, about half of them in Buenos Aires. The U.S. commercial attaché reported that joblessness had reached "the point where it is now a factor seriously disturbing to the political and social life of the country."[73] Most adversely affected were those occupations relating to shipping and construction; both ground almost to complete halts. In 1940, rents rose as a result of property reassessments and the high cost of building materials, and speculators bought up food to create false scarcities. Simultaneously, the government printed more money and inflation became more acute; wages did not keep pace and "the condition of the working class became almost desperate."[74]

The society was a troubled one. Isabel Rennie's diagnosis of a few years later serves well:

> This was the Argentina of June, 1943; disunited, deeply cynical, without purpose or direction. Its spiritual bankruptcy was as patent as its physical prosperity in the war boom, and at the helm of government was a class that no longer had the power to change its direction, or to prevent outside influences from bringing a change of direction. A nation, a society with all its values, was adrift on a wide ocean, with no one to set the course and no one even to point a destination. Argentina had reached the end of an era.[75]

The political and social malaise of the 1930s and early 1940s is reflected in the plethora of nationalistic, and often mutually hostile, groups. In spite of their differences, almost all agreed on a platform combining anti-Semitism, anticommunism, and a rabid aversion to democracy.[76] A new police division, the Special Section for the Repression of Communism, began to combat the political activities of radical groups and to investigate the connection between Jews and communists. In 1936, former Minister of the Interior Matias Sanchez Sorondo published a report that purported to reveal the tentacles of the world communist conspiracy in Argentina and its Jewish allies. Fortunately, the Argentine Congress refused to act on his draconian suggestions to curb left-wing activity.

During the 1930s, anti-Semitism, fueled by French and falangist ideologies, remained the preserve of the oligarchic right. The struggle between nazism and catholicism in Germany prevented the more devout Argentine reactionaries from becoming nazis, although the popular right-wing press quickly adopted a nazi tone.

More important than nazism, though, to the development of right-wing thought in Argentina was Italian fascism. But Mussolini's Argentine admirers were well ahead of him in applying anti-Semitic propaganda. What Gino Germani called "ideological" anti-Semitism already had strong local roots among members of the upper class and needed little nurturing from abroad.[77]

With the exception of some confrontations at the Medical School of the University of Buenos Aires (where an earlier generation of anti-Jewish students had been active during the Tragic Week) and a large volume of hate-filled propaganda, some of it supported by the nazis and by sectors of the Catholic church, the mass of Jews remained objectively unaffected by anti-Semitism. The subjective effects are impossible to gauge, but the tenor of the era doubtless reinforced the Jewish community's perception of its special and precarious place in Argentine society.

The government's position was generally that anti-Semitism arose from a few businessmen and professionals who were jealous of Jewish success. This contention received official expression in a Buenos Aires court in 1939, when a judge refused the request of a Jewish parent to change his son's name from Isaac to Ignacio to shield the boy from anti-Semitism. To grant the petition would have been to admit that Argentine society was, in fact, anti-Semitic.[78]

Another military junta assumed power in March 1943, this one most explicitly anti-Semitic than its predecessors. The group of army officers who masterminded the coup, which included Colonel Juan D. Perón, specifically attacked the masons and the rotarians, both of which it considered Jewish creations. According to the officers, the Rotary Clubs were "a veritable net of espionage and international Jewish propaganda in the service of the United States. . . ."[79] The leaders of the coup also singled out Jews and communists as enemies of the state, supported anti-Semitic publications with official advertising, and decreed compulsory instruction in catholicism. Under this system, children registered as Jewish were segregated from their classmates. The new minister of Justice and Public Instruction, Gustavo Martínez Zuviría, had under the *nom de plume* Hugo Wast made his reputation with best-selling novels that "exposed" the Jewish-communist conspiracy.

The projunta press accused Jews and North American and British capitalists of extracting "profits to the detriment of the financial interest of the nation, . . . thus preventing the nation's economic recovery."[80] In August 1943, the intendant of Buenos Aires issued a decree, largely if not entirely anti-Semitic in conception, that prohibited the kosher preparation of meat in the municipal packing and slaughter houses, holding that it was inconvenient.

On the 16th of August, intelligence received in Washington, D.C., revealed that General Arana, "a notorious pro-Nazi," had ordered the Ministry of Agriculture to compile a list of their Jewish employees so that they could eventually be fired. Other ministries received similar instructions. In an unusual move, President Roosevelt sent the junta a note condemning its anti-Semitic moves. According to North American journalist Ray Josephs, the Argentine regime coerced the president of the Delegación de Asociaciones Israelitas Argentinas (DAIA), the Argentine Jewish antidefamation organization, into signing a letter that "confirmed the certainty that in Argentina there never has been, nor will there ever be, discrimination of a racial, religious, or nationalistic order." At this, Jewish newspapers, which had been closed by government order, asked the international press services not to publicize the action for fear of reprisals sparked by U.S. interference in the domestic affairs of Argentina.[81]

On January 28, 1944, the State Department received a review of anti-Semitic activities that in summary is worth quoting at some length:

> The general trend of anti-Semitism in Argentina has been highlighted by repressive measures carried out against Jewish residents in various parts of Argentina. . . . In October measures were taken against the Jewish language press in Buenos Aires, which resulted in the suspending of several Yiddish papers. . . . Prohibitions were later lifted, and in recent months the government has been less active in the field of anti-Semitic legislation although attitude on the matter remains undefined.
>
> It must be added that there have been many measures passed by the Argentine government which have struck at the Semitic section of the population, even though, on the surface, those measures have not been directed specifically against it. Legislation has been passed which reflects the strong nationalist trend of the Argentine government. This legislation, both social and economic, has made life difficult for all groups without nationalist convictions.[82]

Notes

1. James Bryce, *South America* (New York: Macmillan Co., 1912), p. 320.

2. Sir Thomas Holdich, *The Countries of the King's Award* (London: Hurst and Blackett, Ltd., 1904), pp. 77–78.

3. On the Depression of 1890 and the Baring Brothers crisis, *see:* H.S. Ferns, *Britain and Argentina in the Nineteenth Century* (Oxford: Clarendon Press, 1960); Ysabel Rennie, *The Argentine Republic* (New York: Macmillan Co., 1945); and A.G. Ford, *The Gold Standard, 1880–1914: Britain and Argentina* (Oxford: Clarendon Press, 1962).

4. In 1901, *La Prensa* reported that laborers earned 70 pesos per month while their expenses ran 100 pesos monthly. A middle-class family of five required 250 pesos a month but earned only 150. *See:* James R. Scobie, *Buenos Aires: From Plaza to Suburb* (New York: Oxford University Press, 1974), p. 141.

5. C.E. Akers, *Argentine, Patagonian, and Chilian Sketches* (London: Harrison and Sons, 1893), p. 21.

6. W.H. Koebel, *Argentina: Past and Present* (London: Adam and Charles Black, 1914), p. 56.

7. República Argentina, Departamento Nacional del Trabajo, *Boletín* 21 (November 1912) and Aldo Ferrer, *The Argentine Economy,* trans. Marjorie Urquidi (Berkeley: University of California Press, 1967), p. 116.

8. For the best discussion of the politics of the period, *see:* Rennie, *The Argentine Republic.* On the Socialist party, see Dardo Cuneo, *Juan B. Justo* (Buenos Aires: Editorial Americalee, 1943); Enrique Dickmann, *Recuerdos de un militante socialista* (Buenos Aires: Editorial La Vanguardia, 1949); and José Vazeilles, *Los socialistas* (Buenos Aires: Editorial Jorge Alvarez, 1967). Also *see:* Richard Walter, *The Argentine Socialist Party* (Austin: University of Texas Press, 1977). In 1910, only 20 percent of the total native male population could vote. If immigrants are included only nine percent of the total male population could vote. See: Gino Germani, *Política y sociedad,* pp. 225–226.

9. Bryce, *South America,* p. 341.

10. *American Jewish Year Book,* vol. 54, 1953, p. 202.

11. Juan José Sebreli, *La cuestión judía en la Argentina* (Buenos Aires: Editorial Tiempo Contemporaneo, 1968), pp. 86–90.

12. H. Brusilovsky, "Los judíos en el movimiento obrero," *Homenaje a "El Diario Israelita"* (Buenos Aires: Comite de Homenaje a *El Diario Israelita,* 1940), p. 97. Jewish workers in eastern Europe has been organized into ethnic unions by the Bund. They continued this pattern in the New World for two major reasons. The original inability to communicate in Spanish, and other languages, with coworkers and other cultural differences contributed to a feeling of separateness that was mitigated by a homogeneous union. *See:* "El movimiento gremial," *Juventud,* 6 (July 1916), 74. The second factor to stimulate such unions was a particular nationality's dominance in a given industry. This was the case, for example, of the Jewish capmakers in Buenos Aires. In spite of their organizational homogeneity, Jewish unions in Buenos Aires did not function independently of the major labor federations. Socialists and anarchists recognized the presence and usefulness of Jewish workers and aided them organizationally and with publicity.

13. The Balfour Declaration, issued in 1917, declared that the British government would work to facilitate a National Home for the Jews of Palestine.

14. In addition to its propagandistic and organizational functions, the committee undertook other roles. It promised to deliver as many workers as possible to union assemblies and to have committee members present to explain the aims of the meeting to Jewish workers. The explanations would be in Yiddish to facilitate Jewish participation. It further offered to organize unions in those trades in which Jews constituted a majority of the work force. *See:* Hobart Spalding, *La clase trabajadora argentina* (Buenos Aires: Editorial Galerna, 1970), pp. 432–434. Document drawn from *La Protesta,* March 14, 1908, p. 1. The Committee had the support of all three labor federations. It was active but short lived; splits between the Socialists and the anarchists caused the committee's demise after only six months. *See:* "El movimiento gremial," *Juventud,* 6 (July 1916), 75.

15. *See:* "Los judíos en el socialismo," *Juventud,* 6 (July 1916), 69–73 and Boleslao Lewin, *La colectividad judía en la Argentina* (Buenos Aires: Alzamor Editores, 1974), pp. 118–122.

16. Adrián Patroni, *Los trabajadores en la Argentina* (Buenos Aires: n.p., 1897), p. 88.

On the bakers union, *see:* Sebastián Marotta, *El movimiento sindical Argentino,* vol. 2 (Buenos Aires: Ediciones Lacio, 1961), pp. 21 and 105.

17. On the history of the Bund, *see:* Ezra Mendelsohn, *Class Struggle in the Pale* (Cambridge: Cambridge University Press, 1970); and Henry J. Tobias, *The Jewish Bund in Russia* (Stanford: Stanford University Press, 1972).

18. Ernesto A. Bavio, "Las escuelas extranjeras en Entre Ríos," *El Monitor de educación común,* 27 (November 1908), 597–604 and "Las escuelas extranjeras en Entre Ríos," *El monitor de educación común,* 28 (January 1909), 3–44. *See also:* Carlos O. Bunge, *El espíritu de la educación* (Buenos Aires: n.p., 1901) and Ricardo Rojas, *La restauración nacionalista* (Buenos Aires: Ministerio de Justicia e Instrucción Pública, 1909).

19. Dickmann, *Recuerdos* pp. 158–161.

20. *See:* Osvaldo Bayer, "Simon Radowitzky: mártir o asesino?" *Todo es Historia,* 1 (August 1967), 58–79.

21. John A. Hobson, *The Evolution of Modern Capitalism* (London: George Allen & Unwin, Ltd., 1928), p. 467.

22. Handbills in the possession of IWO, Argentina in Buenos Aires, File #36. *See also:* David Rock, "Machine Politics in Buenos Aires and the Radical Party," *Journal of Latin American Studies,* 4 (November 1972), pp. 233–256.

23. Ernesto Tornquist & Co., Ltd., *The Economic Development of the Argentine Republic in the Last Fifty Years,* (Buenos Aires: Ernesto Tornquist & Co., Ltd., 1919), p. 21; Alejandro E. Bunge, *Los problemas económicos del presente* (Buenos Aires: n.p., 1920), p. 251; United States, Bureau of Labor Statistics, *Monthly Labor Review* (July 1921), 113.

24. Chevrah Keduscha Aschkenasi, *Libros de Actas,* vol. 2 (1910–1917), pp. 230, 264, 279–280, 296, 298.

25. H. Brusilovsky, "Los judíos en el movimiento obrero," and n.a., "El movimiento gremial," *Juventud,* 6 (July 1916), 75, and Pinie Wald, *The Jewish Working Class and Socialist Movement,* (Buenos Aires: A.M.I.A., 1963), p. 16. In Yiddish.

26. Tornquist, *Economic Development,* p. 15; Great Britain, Department of Overseas Trade, *Economic Conditions in the Argentine Republic* (London: H.M. Stationery Office, 1925 and 1931), pp. 71 and 144, respectively.

27. Bunge, *Los problemas económicos,* p. 105.

28. United States, Bureau of Labor Statistics, *Monthly Labor Review* (March 1919), 122.

29. Between 1914 and 1924, the number of work permits issued to minors increased from 5,586 to almost 11,000. United States Bureau of Labor Statistics, *Monthly Labor Review* (December 1925), 94.

30. On the Semana Trágica, *see:* Nicolás Babini, "La semana trágica," *Todo es Historia,* I (September 1967), pp. 8–23; Julio Godio, *La semana trágica de enero 1919* (Buenos Aires: Grancia Editor, 1972); Félix Luna, *Yrigoyen* (Buenos Aires: Editorial Raigal, 1954), pp. 257–258; Sebastián Marotta, *El movimiento sindical argentino,* 2, 241–248; David Rock, "Lucha civil en la Argentina: La semana trágica de enero de 1919," *Desarollo Económico,* 11 (July 1971–March 1972), 165–216; Diego Abad de Santillan, *La F.O.R.A.,* (Buenos Aires: Editorial Proyeccion, 1971), pp. 243–245; and Nahum Solominsky, *La semana trágica* (Buenos Aires: Bilioteca popular judia, 1971). *See also,* IWO, Argentina, File #89.

31. The "counterrevolution" had the strong backing of the military and the Church. The

"patriots" were mostly *criollo*, many of them with a stake in Radical party patronage. Their leaders came from the well-born, several of them long-time political opponents of Irigoyen's. On violence against the community, *see:* Comité de la Colectividad Israelita, *Exposición de atropellos contra instituciones e individuos de la Colectividad Israelita* (Buenos Aires: Comité de la Colectividad Israelita, n.d.). The original is in the possession of IWO, Argentina, File #89. The document is partially reprinted in Lewin, *La colectividad*, p. 128–140.

32. Juan José de Soiza Reilly, "El mártirio de los inocentes," *Revista Popular* (February 1919), vol. 2, n. 42 1–4.

33. José Mendelsohn, "Del Pogrom en Buenos Aires," quoted in Solominsky, *La Semana Trágica,* p. 20.

34. Comité de la Colectividad, *Exposición,* p. 6–7.

35. Frederick J. Stimson, *My United States,* (New York: Charles Scribner's Sons, 1931), pp. 418–421.

36. Quoted in Solominsky, *La Semana Trágica,* pp. 8 and 14.

37. *Di Presse,* February 11, 1919.

38. Federación Sionista Argentina in *Di Yiddishe Zeitung,* January 14, 1919.

39. Poster reproduced in Solominsky, *La Semana Trágica,* p. 29. Original in IWO Archives, Buenos Aires.

40. *La Razón,* January 14, 1919 and *Di Presse,* February 11, 1919.

41. Chevrah Keduscha, *Libro de Actas,* 1917–1923, vol. 3, p. 150.

42. Oscar Cornblit, "European Immigrants in Argentina Industry and Politics," Claudio Veliz, ed., *The Politics of Conformity in Latin America* (New York: Oxford University Press, 1970), p. 221.

43. *See:* Eugene F. Sofer and Mark D. Szuchman, "Educating Immigrants: Voluntary Associations in the Acculturation Process," Thomas J. LaBelle, ed., *Educational Alternatives in Latin America: Social Change and Social Stratification* (Los Angeles: UCLA Latin American Center Publications, 1975), pp. 334–359.

44. Jewish Colonization Association, *Rapport,* 1925, p. 291 and Chevrah Keduscha, *Libros de Actas,* 1917–1923 and *Libros de Actas,* 1926–1929, vol. 5, p. 276.

45. On the Jewish Radical Committee, *see: La Prensa,* February 24, 1918. *El Diario's* report is found in David Rock, "Radicalism," p. 220, f. 610.

46. Partido Israelita Argentino, IWO Archives, File #36.

47. IWO File, Archives of J.S. Liachovitsky.

48. *See:* Luis F. Nuñez, *Los cementerios* (Buenos Aires: Ministerio de Cultura e Educación, 1970), pp. 78–79 and Chevrah Keduscha Aschkenasi, *Libro de Actas,* 1923–1926, vol. 4, p. 234.

49. Chevrah Keduscha, *Libros de Actas,* vol. 3 (1917–1923), pp. 229, 254, 255, 289, 348, 350.

50. On Irigoyen and the British railroads, *see:* Paul B. Goodwin, Jr., "The Politics of Rate-making: the British-owned Railways and the Unión Civica Radical, 1921–1928," *Journal of Latin American Studies,* 6 (November 1974), pp. 257–287. On the development and importance of the YPF, *see:* Robert A. Potash, *The Army and Politics in Argentina,* 1928–1945 (Stanford: Stanford University Press, 1969). Also *see:* Peter Snow, *Argentine Radicalism* (Iowa City: University of Iowa Press, 1965), pp. 34–35.

51. United States, Department of Commerce, *Wearing Apparel in Argentina* (Washington, D.C.: Government Printing Office, 1918), p. 15.

52. United States, Department of Commerce, *Advertising Methods in Argentina, Uruguay and Brazil* (Washington, D.C.: Government Printing Office, 1920), p. 12.

53. United States, Department of Commerce, *The Economic Position of Argentina During the War* (Washington, D.C.: Government Printing Office: 1920), p. 67.

54. Snow, *Argentine Radicalism,* p. 43. *See also:* Félix Luna, *Alvear* (Buenos Aires: Libros Argentinos, 1958), p. 63.

55. United States, Bureau of Labor Statistics, *Monthly Labor Review* (May 1923), 103.

56. United States, Bureau of Labor Statistics, *Monthly Labor Review* (July 1925), 142 and United States, Bureau of Labor Statistics, *Monthly Labor Review* (September 1926), 146.

57. Luna, *Alvear,* p. 64.

58. United States, Bureau of Labor Statistics, *Monthly Labor Review* (September 1926), 175–176 and United States, Bureau of Labor Statistics, *Monthly Labor Review* (October 1972), 202.

59. United States, Bureau of Labor Statistics, *Monthly Labor Review* (December 1929), 229.

60. Chevrah Keduscha, *Libros de Actas,* vol. 4, (1923–1926) pp. 14, 24, 44, and 54.

61. Chevrah Keduscha, *Libros de Actas,* vol. 5, (1926–1929).

62. Vernon L. Phelps, *The International Economic Position of Argentina,* (Philadelphia: University of Pennsylvania Press, 1938), pp. 46–51 and Great Britain, Department of Overseas Trade, *Economic Conditions in the Argentine Republic,* October, 1930 (London: H.M. Stationery Office, 1930), p. 11.

63. *See:* Alberto Ciria, *Partidos y poder en la Argentina moderna* (Buenos Aires: Editorial Jorge Alvarez, 1968); Alberto Ciria, et. al. *La década infame* (Buenos Aires: Carlos Perez Editor, 1969); Ronald H. Dolkart, "Manual A. Fresco, Governor of the Province of Buenos Aires, 1936–1940," (Los Angeles: unpublished doctoral dissertation, UCLA, 1969); Rodolfo Puiggros, *La democracia fraudulenta* (Buenos Aires: Editorial Jorge Alvarez, 1968); and Rennie, *The Argentine Republic.*

64. José Panettieri, *Síntesis histórica del desarollo industrial argentino* (Buenos Aires: Sintesís historica, 1969), pp. 80–83.

65. United States, Bureau of Labor Statistics, *Monthly Labor Review* (March 1934), 749–750.

66. Great Britain, Department of Overseas Trade, *Economic Conditions in the Argentine Republic,* October 1930, p. 91.

67. United States, Bureau of Labor Statistics, *Monthly Labor Review* (January 1933), 78. Unfortunately, it is quite difficult to determine what percentage of the work force was idle in 1932. No census was taken until 1935 when the government commissioned an industrial census that excluded all agricultural laborers. A parallel census for agriculture was conducted in 1937. In 1935, 419,133 adult males made a living in industry. In 1937, 1,193,344 males either operated agricultural holdings or worked on them. Adding the two, we get a total of 1,612,477 employed males. In 1932, there were 316,556 unemployed males. Assuming for the moment that the same number of people worked in 1932 as in 1935 and 1937, unemployment among Argentine males would have been 19.6 percent. The fact, of course, is that the work force was smaller in 1932, which strongly indicates that unemployment may have affected 25 percent

of the employed male population. *See:* República Argentina, Comisión nacional del censo industrial. *Censo industrial de 1935* (Buenos Aires: Jacobo Peuser, 1938) and Felix Weil, *The Argentine Riddle* (New York: John Day Co., 1944), appendix C, Table II,. p. 265.

68. Chevrah Keduscha, *Libros de Actas,* vol. 7, 1932–1936, pp. 102–103.

69. Chevrah Keduscha, *Libros de Actas,* vol. 7, 1931–1936, p. 69.

70. Ciria, *Partidos y poder,* p. 277.

71. Great Britain, Department of Overseas Trade, *Economic Conditions in the Argentine Republic,* January, 1933. (London: H. M. Stationery Office, 1933), p. 41.

72. The Roca-Runciman pacts stimulated nationalist sentiment in Argentina. *See:* Mark Falcoff, "Raul Scalabrini Ortiz"; Marysa Gerassi, *Los nacionalistas;* (Buenos Aires: Editorial Jorge Alvarez, 1969); and Peter H. Smith, *Politics & Beef in Argentina* (New York: Columbia University Press, 1969), pp. 137–169.

73. United States, Bureau of Labor Statistics, *Monthly Labor Review* (May 1941), pp. 1123–1125.

74. Rennie, *The Argentine Republic,* p. 304.

75. Ibid., p. 342.

76. *See:* Falcoff, "Raul Scalabrini Ortiz" pp. 74–101; Marysa Gerassi, "Argentine Nationalism of the Right," (New York: unpublished doctoral dissertation, Columbia University, 1964); and Gerassi, *Los nacionalistas.* Falcoff offers the interesting distinction between aristocratic nationalists and popular nationalists. "For the popular nationalist, the 'un-Argentine' elements in society were not the immigrants, the Jews or the Freemasons (favorite targets of the aristocratic nationalists), but the scions of distinguished families, prototypically portrayed as lawyers for foreign firms or their pawns in national politics. Popular nationalism thus offered the Argentine middle class the gratifying possibility of pursuing its own corporate interests—social mobility, economic opportunity, political influence—within the framework of a crusade for national sovereignty," p. 78.

77. Gino Germani, "Antisemitismo ideologico y antisemitismo tradicional," Torcuato S. Di Tella and Tulio Halperin, eds., *Los Fragmentos del poder* (Buenos Aires: Editorial Jorge Alvarez, 1969), pp. 461–476.

78. *American Jewish Year Book,* vol. 42, 1940–1941, p. 429.

79. United States, Department of State, November 13, 1945. R. 6.59, 1945–1949, box 5444, file 835.00/11–145–11–1545.

80. United States, Department of State, confidential, Buenos Aires, June 14, 1943, R. 6.59, 1940–1944. box 4051, file 835.00/1551–1616.

81. Ray Josephs, *Argentine Diary* (New York: Random House, 1944), pp. 185–186.

82. United States, Department of State, January 28, 1944, R.6.59, 1940–1944, box 4054, file 835.00/2293–2392.

CHAPTER 4

THE CITY

In the three decades between 1880 and 1910, ambitious *porteños* laid the foundation for modern Buenos Aires. Revenues from agricultural exports permitted them to expand basic services, survey and pave new streets and avenues, beautify parks, and begin building modern port facilities. The Plaza de Mayo, fronting the Executive Mansion, was even carved out at the expense of the city's colonial town hall. In 1894, workers began work on the Avenida de Mayo, perhaps the single most famous street in Buenos Aires. Early in the twentieth century, the Colon Opera, the *porteños* monument to culture, and the aptly named Palace of Justice both rose as evidence of Argentina's wealth. By the time these herculean efforts had been completed, proud *porteños* called their city the "Paris of South America."[1]

But not all of Buenos Aires was beautified. Around the turn of the century, immigrants and tourists both registered little better than horror at their first impressions of the city. And no wonder. "First the traveller was lowered from the ship onto a wretched little tender, . . . then from the tender he was transferred to a small boat which, if there was sufficient water, would take him to the mole stairs or, if not, would carry him as far as the water reached, and then the rest of the journey ashore would be performed either on the shoulders of an uncouth Italian, or in a heavy springless cart, with wheels eight or nine feet in diameter." First meetings with the authorities also left vivid memories: ". . . when at last we escaped from the *aduana* [customs house] and made our way to the nearest refreshment bar, I was in that state of mind in which the predominant feeling is a miserable doubt as to whether after all, life is worth living. . . ."[2] While we can only imagine how much worse immigrants felt after a trans-Atlantic crossing in far worse conditions, modernization of the port and improved public health measures to combat epidemics eventually made coming to Buenos Aires less dangerous.

By 1900, Buenos Aires was becoming a city of incredible dynamism. Its population increased by tens of thousands yearly, and new neighborhoods sprung up to house immigrants and natives alike. New industries appeared, offering fresh opportunities for workers, employees, and managers. In contrast to this activity, however, was a certain stasis. *Barrios* (neighborhoods) assumed the characteristics of a given social class, retained them, and in doing so bred the notion that people did not move extensively within the city's limits.

In the first half of the twentieth century, a number of factors restricted geographic mobility between the neighborhoods of Buenos Aires. Income, residential segregation—sometimes conscious, sometimes not—and the distance between home and job, all combined to limit unrestrained movement. Commercial factors, in particular the requisites of the artisanal form of production, also encouraged people not to move.

Nevertheless there are four identifiable stages in the residential history of Jews in Buenos Aires between 1890 and 1947. Each is a distinct stage in the community's evolution, and each also represents a stage in the history of Jewish ghettoization. The first is entry and the search for institutional and spatial stability; the second, ghettoization and unity; the third, second-stage ghettoization and westward movement; and the fourth, dispersion and the fragmentation of the community.

STAGE ONE: ARRIVAL

In 1895, 62 percent of the Ashkenazi Jews in the city lived around Plaza Lavalle, the future site of the Palace of Justice. While there were significant clusters of Jews in District 6 and near the port, only a few lived in the city's six westernmost districts (see Figures 1 and 2).

In the first stage of its evolution, the Plaza Lavalle was the center of the Jewish community. Located between *calles* (streets) Lavalle, Viamonte, Libertad, and Talcahuano, the area for years housed the city's older western European Jewish colony. The Plaza was also the site of an informal outdoor labor exchange, reminiscent of the "chazar mart" of New York City's Lower East Side. (The name is Yiddish for pig market, which conveys a sense of the indignities involved in finding a job.)[3]

Largely because of these attractions, the Plaza was an obvious haven for immigrants. In the late nineteenth and early twentieth centuries, new Jewish immigrants beat a path from the Immigrant Hotel to the Plaza. There they met coreligionists, acquainted themselves with their new surroundings, and sought work, at first from the more established Sephardim (western European Jews), and later from the more

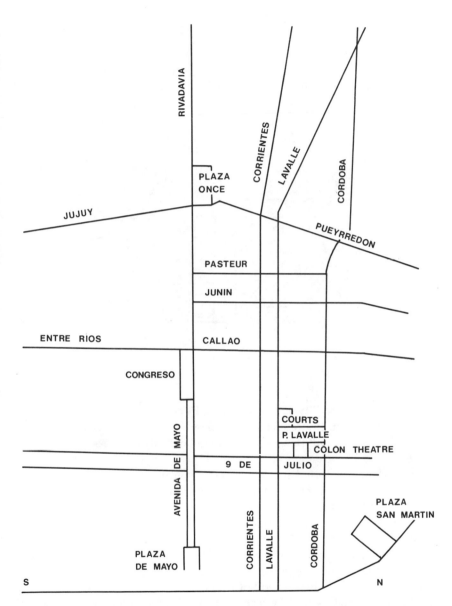

Figure 1. Buenos Aires from the Avenida de Mayo North, 1890–1945.

successful Ashkenazim.[4] The Plaza also housed the Congregación Israelita, which in 1897 built a synagogue at Libertad 785. This area had
already become the Jewish community's main commercial thor-
oughfare. Small stores, rented by pawnbrokers and second-hand

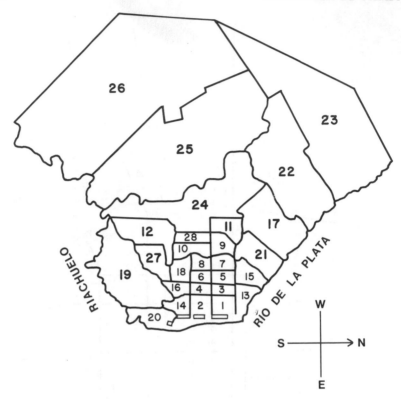

Figure 2. The City of Buenos Aires, by census district, in 1895.
After 1895, the city reduced the number of census districts. The old
districts and the new ones are not directly comparable.

clothes dealers, dotted its sidewalks.[5] Overall, the neighborhood was
extremely heterogeneous, serving as a center for prostitution as well as
religion and commerce.

By 1895, three of the four census districts around the Plaza registered densities of more than 200 people per hectare.[6] Crowding was
caused as much by a lack of housing as by significant population
growth, but neither the prospect of overcrowding nor economic crises
could stem the northward tide of *porteños*.

Those districts in which most Jews lived contained less than 10
percent of the buildings in Buenos Aires in 1895. Some 43 percent of
the buildings in these areas were foreign owned, but only two of the
eight Russian Jews who owned property in 1895—José Blitz, a physi-
cian, and Soly Borok, a bed manufacturer—had holdings in these
areas. The other Jewish landowners, three merchants, a cigarette

maker, a peon, and a farmer resided and owned property in neighborhoods even less desirable than the area around the Plaza.[7]

Citywide, one-story buildings on the colonial pattern predominated, but the number of two-story buildings increased rapidly in
the years before 1890. The 1895 census even counted almost 1,000
buildings of three or more floors. The dynamism of the north side of
Buenos Aires was reflected in brick and stone, which signified progress
as well as better protection against the elements. Jews lived in housing
that was typical of their districts.[8]

Population growth severely exacerbated the housing crisis in
Buenos Aires. Between 1869 and 1895, the city's population grew some
225 percent, while available housing increased only 163 percent. In this
regard, the oligarchy's heightened sense of civic responsibility brought
mixed blessings to the overcrowded city. Between 1887 and 1892, municipal authorities ordered the demolition of 2,000 dwellings. Some
were destroyed because they were particularly unsanitary; others had
to go to make room for public buildings, for the Avenida de Mayo and
other major thoroughfares, and later for Parisian style diagonals. Such
urban renewal increased the opportunities for new construction in
housing, but relatively little building took place.[9]

Official inactivity and the preferences of investors contributed to the
housing shortage. Those with surplus capital preferred to speculate in
land rather than invest in housing. Nor was the construction industry,
which lacked equipment, technology, and skilled labor, able to meet
demand. The high cost of raw materials further stemmed the en-
thusiasm of potential builders. The use of residences in the center city
for commercial purposes exacerbated the crisis because it reduced
housing stock. Finally, the 1890 depression put an end to both speculation and construction for about a decade. Although by 1900 well-to-do
porteños had again begun to invest in urban housing, the housing stock
continued to decline relative to the skyrocketing number of potential
renters.

STAGE TWO: THE GHETTO

It was not long before the Jewish community began to move west
from the Plaza Lavalle to barrio Once, named after the 11 de Sep-
tiembre railroad station. Here it embarked on the second stage of its
residential history: ghettoization and unity. The reasons for this abrupt
demographic shift are not difficult to determine. In the aftermath of the
yellow fever epidemic of 1871, the porteño elite began to move north to

higher, more sanitary ground. The migration gathered momentum, and after 1910 the construction of ornate public and private edifices caused a steep increase in the cost of the land north of the Avendia de Mayo. Between 1904 and 1912, the price of a square meter of land in the parish of San Nicolás increased from 133.3 pesos to 998.5 pesos, a factor of increase of 7.5. In the same period, the price of land in the western districts, which included *barrio* Once, increased slightly more than half as much.[10] The Jewish community, unable to pay the higher rents the more expensive land commanded, was driven to less densely populated and less desirable areas away from the city's expanding commercial, official, and residential core.

By 1900, the Avenida de Mayo had inalterably divided Buenos Aires into north and south. The population north of the avenue, which included most of the city's Jews, soon came to see the avenue "as a barrier to movement to the southern commercial districts, which quickly declined as pedestrian traffic south of the avenue fell off." The Avenida de Mayo "sharply divided the barrios of the north from those of the south. Behind this wall the colonial barrios stagnated, . . . and their commerce vegetated painfully."[11]

As Socialist deputy Mario Bravo described the city about a decade later:

> We have a city divided in two: the city of the north and the city of the south; the city of wealthy barrios and that of poor barrios; the well lit streets and that of the streets without lights; the hygienic city and the city that lately received the benefits of public cleanliness, for which they pay, nevertheless; the barrios where the mortality is 17.6 per thousand as in the working class section of San Bernardo, and where it is 9.75 per thousand, as in the well kept parish of Socorro; barrios protected against the advance of the tides and barrios occupied by extensive, uninhabited landholdings and barrios where the population must gather itself in miserable hovels and in horrible conventillos.[12]

Although most Jews did live in the northern half of the city, they were centered considerably to the west of the city's thriving core. Still, by following the western European Jews into what had been the less desirable north side, the eastern European Jews eventually derived certain benefits; in time they found themselves in the midst of neighborhoods changing for the better.

During the second stage of the Jewish community's history in Buenos Aires, between approximately 1907 and 1925, Once was stamped as the most important Jewish residential and commercial neighborhood in the city. The community's institutions took root in

Once and, in terms of visible symbols of ethnicity, the neighborhood became distinctly Jewish.

In *barrio* Once, Jews established what amounted to a ghetto that protected them. Daily life was conducted along traditional lines, and familiar institutions tended to mitigate the harshness of acculturation. The Once ghetto owed its existence to affordable rents, to cultural affinity, and to the proximity of labor to potential employment. Institutions—religious, educational, recreational, commercial, and hygienic—ordered every day life in the community, helping its Jewish residents adapt to Argentine realities.[13]

The ghetto in Buenos Aires was never defined by physical barriers erected to keep Jews within stone walls. Rather, it was the result of often subtle economic factors and equally subtle decisions made by its inhabitants. In Louis Wirth's classic and still valid formulation, the modern ghetto "is no longer the place of officially regulated settlement of the Jews, but rather a local cultural area which has arisen quite informally." The traditional European ghetto, on the other hand, was a "densely populated walled-in area usually found near the arteries of commerce or in the vicinity of a market. . . . A common factor of all ghettoes was the cemetery, a communal responsibility to which unusual sentiment was attached." There were also "a number of educational, recreational, and hygienic institutions. . . . In the close life within the ghetto walls almost nothing was left to the devices of the individual. Life was well-organized, often verging on overorganization. These institutions did not appear ready made. They represent what life always is, an adaptation to the physical and social needs of a people."

The ghetto walls have long since disappeared in most countries, and they never did appear in Argentina. Nevertheless "an invisible wall of isolation still maintains the distance between the Jew and his neighbors."[14] As Wirth points out, the ghetto owes its existence to more than religious prejudice:

> Even for those who are indifferent to religious observances and ritual, . . . residence in the ghetto is necessitated by social and economic circumstances. Ignorance of the language of the new country, of its labour conditions, and of its general habits and ways of thought, as well as the natural timidity of a fugitive, . . . compels the immigrant Jew to settle in the colony of his co-religionists. Among them he is perfectly at home; he finds the path of employment comparatively smooth, and if his efforts to attain it be delayed, he is helped in the interval by charity from a dozen hands.[15]

Although Jews were slightly more segregated in 1895 than subse-

quently, the appearance of the ghetto in Once resulted in the matura-
tion of the community's institutions, forming the second of its four
historical stages.

The basic institutional structure of the Jewish ghetto in Buenos
Aires developed on the eastern European model. The Chevrah opened
in 1895 and, thanks to the efforts of its president, Nahum Enquin,
purchased the land for its first cemetery in Liniers, Buenos Aires Province, in 1910. Jews also founded an orphan asylum, an old age home, a
Jewish hospital, and a variety of other voluntary associations.

New Jewish immigrants, conscious of their inability to speak
Spanish, derived comfort from Yiddish newspapers and magazines.
Indeed, the more assimilated Jewish youth, educated in Argentina,
sought to translate the rhetoric of the Argentine labor movement into
Yiddish. Many Jews taught themselves Spanish; Jewish medical students and other university students offered night school classes in
Spanish, Argentine history, and Argentine geography.[16] Yiddish continued, however, to dominate the community through the 1930s, even
though its use in public gatherings was outlawed during the infamous
decade.

The Chevrah differed in important and instructive ways from its
counterparts in New York and London. The Chevrah in Buenos Aires
soon came to be dominated by immigrants. But though most of its
officers were successful businessmen, the institution remained an integral part of the community. In contrast, London's Board of Guardians
antedated the mass migration from eastern Europe, and control of the
Board effectively remained in the hands of prominent Anglo-Jewish
families like the Montefiores and Rothschilds.[17] The New York Kehillah enjoyed some initial success but quickly declined in importance as
it became less relevant to immigrant needs.[18]

The synagogue was a far more important institution in London and
in New York than in Buenos Aires. Jews emigrated to Argentina when
"the battle against traditionalism and against the religious establishment in Russia and Poland was at its height, and even those who had
not risen to revolt whilst still in Europe considered it in order 'to throw
away their tefilin [phylacteries]' on reaching the shores of Argentina."[19] Shops remained open on the Sabbath, employers paid workers
on Saturday, and the offices of the Jewish Colonization Association,
which might have been expected to provide an example to the community, remained open until two in the afternoon every Saturday.[20] If the
founders of the journal *Juventud* are any example, the first generation
of Jews to be educated in Argentina had "long [been] divorced from
affairs of heaven."[21] In the absence of effective competition from the
synagogue, the Chevrah remained central to community affairs.

The population movement that characterized the Jewish community until 1910 should be understood as a failure to establish a lasting community around the Plaza Lavalle. Poor Jewish immigrants simply could not withstand the expansion of the city's core. The move to *barrio* Once, beginning between 1900 and 1910, was consolidated between 1914 and 1930. An index of dissimilarity, used to measure the degree of residential segregation in a given area, reveals that by 1909 even the city's English population, generally regarded as especially closed and tightknit, was only slightly more than half as segregated as the Jewish population.[22]

By 1904, 56 percent of the Jewish community lived in districts 11 and 14; although clusters of Jewish residences in La Boca and Barracas (districts 3 and 4), south of the Avenida de Mayo, persisted. District 9 housed about 200 Jews, most of whom lived in the northern half of the zone. Although Jews actually formed only a small minority of those who lived between Cordoba on the north, Rivadavia on the south, Pueyrredon on the west, and the port, certain areas, densely populated with Jews, comprised a ghetto. In the five years bctween 1904 and 1909, the Jewish population in district 9 increased tenfold. The number of Jews in district 11 increased 360 percent, while the Jewish population of district 14 grew by only 130 percent. By 1914, almost 40 percent of the city's eastern European population lived in districts 9 or 11, representing a significant shift away from the central business district.

Overcrowding, at least partially occasioned by changes in land use, is characteristic of all ghettoes, and those districts in which Jews lived continued to reflect the crowding north of the Avenida de Mayo.[23] In 1904, for example, districts 9, 11, and 14 registered population densities of 227, 291, and 227 people per hectare, respectively.[24] In 1909 some 4,000 Russian Jews lived in a two-block area in district 11 (see Figure 3).[25] Most Jews continued to reside in one-story buildings. A study of building use revealed that almost half were occupied by families, about a fifth by families and businesses, and five percent by businesses or workshops. One in every four buildings in Buenos Aires was a single-family home.[26]

Census data show that between 1909 and the outbreak of World War I, districts 9, 11, and 14 increased in population by between 8.8 and 14 percent, while the population of district 15 increased 123 percent. Intriguingly, the number of buildings in the three "Jewish" districts declined between 1909 and 1914, probably the result of census inaccuracies.

For the city as a whole, between 1904 and 1909 the population increased from 945,000 to 1,200,000. The directors of the municipal census noted that "to appreciate the magnitude of this increase it is

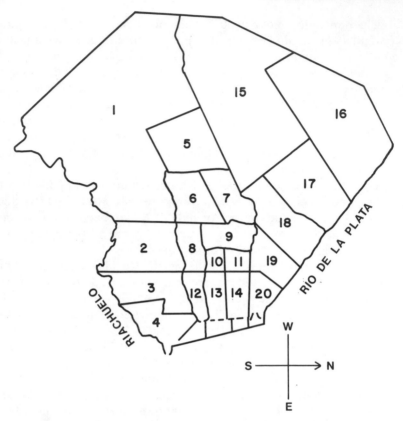

Figure 3. The City of Buenos Aires, by census district, in 1904–1947.
Districts with concentrations of Jews include 9, 11, 14, and 15.

necessary to remember that in the last five years, due to the division of
large parcels of land situated in villages or towns near the Capital into
lots, facilities for their acquisition on installments and the advantages
offered by local trains or electric tramways, a considerable number of
residents, principally in the working class, have left the city to live in
the surrounding towns."[27]

As *porteños* took advantage of the seemingly limitless land to the
west, the city experienced significant spatial expansion in the first three
decades of the century. Between 1895 and 1914, for instance, the south-
westernmost section of Vélez Sársfield (district 1 in Figure 3) increased in population from 4,500 to more than 100,000. Belgrano,
incorporated into Buenos Aires in 1887, grew from 15,000 in 1895 to
almost 230,000 in 1936, while Flores, also annexed in 1887, grew tenfold between 1895 and 1936. Improved rail transportation, trolleys, the

automobile, and the relatively inexpensive prices charged for land made the urban fringe more attractive, although these areas lagged behind the central city in providing basic services.

Despite the abundant open space on the city's rural and under-populated periphery, rents in Buenos Aires continued to rise dramatically. Forty-three percent of the buildings in district 14 and 38 percent in district 11 rented for between 300 and 500 pesos per month. In district 9, 42 percent cost between 50 pesos and 150 pesos a month.[28]

In the aftermath of a tenants' strike in 1907, the Argentine Department of Labor tried to explain constantly rising rents to the city's renters. Most important, officials insisted, was that new construction had not kept pace with population growth. Taxes, scarce labor, expensive raw materials, and relatively high wages also contributed to steep building costs. As the value of land increased, landlords charged higher rents. Because workers were tied by their jobs and the high cost of commuting to the central city, they had few alternatives.[29]

By all accounts, speculation mania gripped prosperous *porteños* in the first decade of the twentieth century. According to the U.S. Department of Commerce:

> Property values rose to quotations hitherto unknown and far in excess of their actual worth. Dealing in land became a sort of craze, and . . . everyone possessed property or papers supposedly representing it. Both buying and selling operations were carried on feverishly. Then suddenly, in 1913, the bubble burst. Thousands of people were caught with holdings obtained at fabulous prices which were worth nothing at all in hard cash. Where money was available it could buy the finest properties for considerably under their real value. Thousands were ruined and speculation ceased abruptly. Even legitimate purchases began to fall off and retrenchment became the rule in all lines.[30]

Roger Babson, a visitor from the United States, made the same observations. Between 1907 and 1909, he said, "lands were booming and prices were higher than . . . in the United States. Since then [1916] there has been a drop of thirty to forty percent, so that now prices—although perhaps not low—are reasonable. . . ."[31]

The extensive emigration that accompanied World War I fortunately reduced the pressure on the housing market, at least temporarily. In this sense, too, the war was a safety valve for Argentina because between 1910 and 1916 the value of new construction in Buenos Aires declined more than 90 percent.[32] Between 1915 and 1917, rents fell for the only time in the four decades after 1890.

This period of deflating real rents did not last for long. On the city's

periphery, population growth prompted a second epidemic of speculation, this time coupled with increased construction, between 1918 and
the mid-1920s. Crucial to this phenomenon was a monthly payment
plan that allowed speculators and potential homeowners to buy land on
liberal credit terms. The manipulation of these terms to exclude low-
income buyers and the higher costs that marked life on the periphery
tended to reinforce, rather than ease, residential segregation. Workers
could not easily afford the monthly payments, the cost of construction,
or the journey to work on public transportation.

Those who chose, or were forced, to stay in the city also faced
rapidly increasing rents. By 1921, rents had far surpassed their prewar
levels; rents for rooms were up by 69 percent, for three-room houses
by 41 percent, and for four-room dwellings by 30 percent.[33]

A 1920 report graphically described the nature of the crisis.

> With land values as high as $85 (U.S. currency) per square foot in the
> central parts of Buenos Aires and single story houses the prevailing type,
> rents are necessarily high. A five room flat, exclusive of kitchen, suitable
> for the average mechanic, rents for $60 per month, or actually more than
> his month's wages. Consequently several large families often occupy a
> single house, and even so there are cases of eviction because of inability
> to pay rent.[34]

Between 1920 and 1925 rents for tenement apartments rose some
50 percent. At the end of this period, renters suffered a significant
defeat when the Supreme Court declared a municipal rent-control law
passed in 1920, and extended by President Alvear in 1923 and 1924,
unconstitutional. In the course of its brief but stormy history, the ordi-
nance had been challenged three times and extended twice.

The original legislation prevented landlords from raising rents
above the rates in effect on January 1, 1920. It also prohibited all
eviction proceedings under certain conditions. A second measure
nullified any clauses that excluded children in all leases. Whenever
Alvear's extensions of the law expired, tenants charged that landlords
immediately raised rents and started to evict tenants. As a result, the
law was continually extended, remaining in effect until the court
handed down its decision.[35] After that, owners raised rents even more
frequently and arbitrarily, threatening tenants with the possibility of
eviction. Couples with children found it more difficult to find housing
than the single and childless. These characteristics of the housing market greatly stimulated residential mobility.

The rental system also might as well have been designed to prey on unsuspecting immigrants. It was the "custom to place the address of a house to be rented with a rental agent who charges a fee of 10 pesos [$4.30] to the prospective tenant before he gives the address of a vacant apartment. This means that a person looking for a flat often spends 50 to 60 pesos . . . for information before suitable accommodations are found."[36]

High rents were the bane of all *porteños*. One contemporary reported that "the prevailing rents in and around Buenos Aires are probably as high, if not higher than, any city in the world."[37] While rents tended to decrease as one moved from the central business district, such a move was counterbalanced by inferior services and transportation problems. Out-migration was the answer for some, but as Socialist Deputy Enrique Dickmann observed in a comprehensive critique, it was certainly no panacea. "The classic lot of seven meters by sixty meters is one of the gravest inconveniences for construction in Buenos Aires. It is essential to develop large, collective, inexpensive and comfortable houses. On the other hand, to construct single homes, one must travel far, to the suburbs, thus separating the working class, and a numerous group of employees, from their workplaces in this great city. . . ." Dickmann also condemned real estate speculation: "one of the gravest evils of housing in the city of Buenos Aires has been . . . the sale by auction of these small lots of land, which speculation has greatly stimulated, and that have subsequently been built on without any plan or method, whatsoever." As a result, he concluded, "there is housing in the suburbs and on the outskirts which is bad, [indeed] terrible, and in lamentable conditions of health and hygiene."[38]

The kind of housing available to most *porteños* was often as serious a problem as its cost. Those who did not live in what the municipality judged to be tenements or in single-family dwellings (usually elite residences, if located in the central business district), lived in small apartment buildings, multifamily units, or boardinghouses of dubious quality. Facing the prospect of class conflict as a result of the city's overcrowded, unsanitary, and crime-ridden housing, the oligarchy started to pay more attention to the "social question" in the second decade of this century. The city, and then the central government, began to play more active roles in the construction and regulation of housing. Both levels of government, occasionally in conjunction with the private sector, tried to alleviate the housing shortage by supporting, or building, working-class housing. In spite of their good intentions, neither official nor private sponsors made a dent in the problem.[39] The municipality was also remiss in improving the existing stock of housing.

A small construction boom in 1929 and 1930 stimulated a 20 percent reduction of rents for small apartments in the first months of 1931. But most rents remained uninterruptedly high; so high that "the average laborer finds his wages unequal to the task of providing the necessities for his family."[40]

One compromise with high rents, especially widespread among Buenos Aires' Jews, was to use the residence as a workplace. Thus, in 1909, the mixed use of property in areas of high Jewish concentration was anywhere from 9 to 23 percent higher than in Buenos Aires as a whole. At the same time, there were 5 to 16 percent fewer apartments and between 6 and 17 percent fewer single-family homes than in other districts.[41]

If Jews did not work in the same building in which they lived, their jobs were almost always close to their homes. From the first years of massive Jewish immigration to Buenos Aires, employment more than any factor except culture, dictated where Jews lived. "Most immigrants were largely restricted to central residental districts until either a rise in incomes allowed them to move to the suburbs, or until public monies subsidized rent payments. . . . Many immigrants were employed in occupations with long and awkward hours, and therefore, preferred a short pedestrian journey to work. . . . Employment in the central business district had the advantage of a wide range of alternative opportunities when regular work was abruptly terminated."[42]

The constraints of employment were again a factor as the Jewish community began to form ghettoes, particularly in *Barrio* Once. Immigrants often comprised the majority of the labor force in specific trades, which encouraged them to live in areas where employment from countrymen was available. Analysis of the location of Jewish businesses verifies the importance of the relationship between home and job.[43] The data clearly show the decline in commercial importance after 1914 of the area around the Plaza Lavalle as Once became both the residential choice of Jews and the center of Jewish entrepreneurship and employment. In 1917, fully one-third of the traceable members of the Chevrah worked in the center city. Over the course of the next decade, that percentage declined to one-fifth, while 41 percent of all Chevrah members worked in Once.

Very incomplete information for 1917 and 1921 shows that between 55 and 88 percent of all the traceable sample members lived and worked at the same address or on the same block. In 1927, the number of Jews who lived and worked at the same address or on the same block significantly outnumbered those who lived more than a block away from where they were employed. In 1927, between half and three-quarters of all those traced lived and worked in the same district. These percentages rise consistently and reflect the residential and commercial dimensions of the consolidation of the Jewish petty bourgeoisie. The more recently a nonmanual occupation was achieved, the more likely a sample member was to live and work in the same district.[44]

STAGE 3: THE MOVE WEST

Most Jews remained near the central city, in *barrio* Once or elsewhere, until 1914. Coinciding with the turmoil caused by World War I, though, concentrations of Jews appeared in districts 7 and 15, indicating a continued westward migration. Census district 15, forming a large part of the *barrio* of Villa Crespo, soon came to house the single largest segment of the Jewish community.

The shift was clearly underway by 1920. Almost 15 percent of those who joined the Chevrah in that year lived in Villa Crespo. In contrast, less than three percent of those who joined the association between 1905 and 1910 lived in Villa Crespo when they enrolled. A comparison of sample members' addresses before and when they joined the Chevrah in 1920 also shows the growing popularity of Villa Crespo. By the time they joined the Chevrah, the percentage of Jews living in Villa Crespo had jumped from five to 15 percent, while those living in Once increased only slightly.[45]

Buenos Aires changed in many ways between 1900 and 1936. Technological improvements facilitated the diffusion of population into newly urbanized areas, and Buenos Aires incorporated suburbs like Flores and Belgrano. Electrified tramways replaced the horse drawn street cars of the 1870s. Between 1912 and 1914, laborers completed the first of five subway lines, this one running beneath the Avenida de Mayo and Calle Rivadavia. Jews, however, at least until the 1930s, rarely took advantage of these improvements and remained in the older sections of the city.

By 1936, some 30,000 Jews, about 25 percent of the city's total Jewish population, lived in Villa Crespo. Villa Crespo did not exactly conform to the general idea of a second-stage ghetto where the traditional symbols of isolation become muted, because Jewish immigrants from Poland settled there. Thus, Villa Crespo, a *barrio* that first took shape at the end of the nineteenth century, performed two functions for *porteño* Jews in the twentieth century. For Russian Jews, it represented a move from Once, the ghetto they had striven to create after being pushed from the central business district. For Polish Jews, Villa Crespo played a role similar to the one that the Plaza Lavalle played for Russian Jews. The area drew newcomers to it because of its cultural affinity, affordable rents, and jobs. For the Polish Jews, Villa Crespo was the first-stage ghetto.

The pattern of living and working in the same immediate area followed the Jewish migration to Villa Crespo. By 1927, the percentage of Jews working in Villa Crespo had grown to 12 percent from two percent in 1917. Reflecting the initial phases to residential dispersion, the percentage of Jews working in scattered districts increased from 12 to 21 percent. By 1936, only 14 percent of the traceable sample members worked in the center city, one third worked in Once, 13 percent worked in Villa Crespo, 14 percent worked on the periphery, and 18 percent worked in various neighborhoods throughout the city (see Figure 4). Data for the 1930 sample reveal that 68 percent of the sample members lived and worked in the same district. By 1936, the percentage was even higher, being between 65 and 81 percent.

Villa Crespo's Jewish population continued to grow between the mid-1920s and 1936, but to *porteños* the ghetto remained in Once. Even in the 1940s, Calle Corrientes, Once's main artery, hummed with activity. Small stores sold textiles and ready-to-wear clothing, grocery stores catered to Jewish tastes, and stores advertised in Yiddish as well as in Spanish.

Once also housed Jewish theatres, banks, credit organizations, and the community's religious and voluntary associations. On Lavalle, parallel to Corrientes, one could "stumble across rabbis, cantors, Hebrew teachers, ritual slaughterers, and hear the buzzing of a Jewish bible class, and see . . . the other characteristics of Jewish holidays."[46] That at least some businesses closed on Saturday to observe the Jewish sabbath added to the *barrio's* ethnic flavor. Old *barrio* Once, the nineteenth-century home of oxcarts, the Corrales de Miserere, and warehouses, had disappeared. Over the span of six decades *barrio* Once had given its name to a readily identifiable ethnic ghetto in the middle of Buenos Aires.[47]

The persistence of the ghetto through the 1940s obscures the fact that Jews changed dwellings with great frequency. Among those Jews enumerated in the 1895 census, for example, the percentage of those living in Once remained more or less constant between 1917 and 1936 (about one third). However, 83 percent of them moved at least once, 40 percent moved twice, and 13 percent moved four or more times. Most of the mobility took place within the confines of the ghetto. Among those Jews who joined the Chevrah between 1905 and 1910, about 45

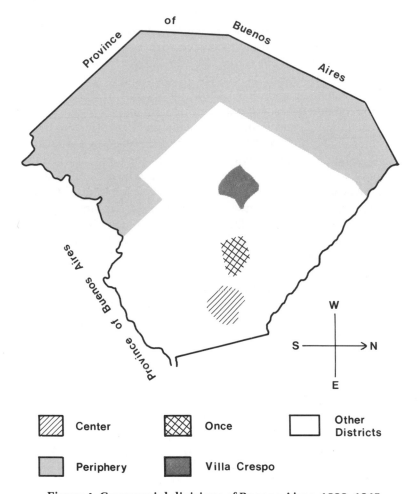

Figure 4. Commercial divisions of Buenos Aires, 1890–1945

percent remained in Once between 1927 and 1936. The amount of mobility, however, was truly startling. Some 69 percent moved five times, and 11.2 percent changed residences as many as ten times during their lives.

Unfortunately, information is so scarce that it is difficult to explain why someone like Marcos B. moved fourteen times between 1909 and his death in 1936 at the age of seventy-nine. He was a bookbinder, and like his colleagues in the working class tended to move more frequently than Jews who worked in nonmanual occupations. It is likely that family size, changes in the life cycle, and poverty contributed to this sort of movement, but at present there is no way of knowing for sure.

What can be said with certainty is that while the ethnicity of the ghetto remained unchanged, significant population movement, probably unseen by the average Argentine, occurred within it.

Although 44.3 percent of the 1914–15 sample lived in Once when they joined the Chevrah, 11 percent of the sample moved from the ghetto between 1921 and 1927. About 60 percent of the Jews in this sample moved five times, but only four percent moved ten times during their lives. Jaime Z. and Jaime K. were distinct exceptions to the rule. The former, a shoemaker, moved a dozen times between August 1915 and 1944, when he apparently dropped out of the Chevrah. The latter, who identified himself as a worker in 1914 but whose family listed him as a street vendor when he died in 1956, moved ten times. More common were Najim O., a woodworker who moved five times during his 35-year membership in the Chevrah, and prominent Jewish attorney Isaac Nissensohn, who moved four times between 1914 and his death in 1963. The lawyer and the woodworker had one other thing in common; each last lived in the home of a son.

In 1920, 44 percent of those who joined the Chevrah lived in Once; only one-third of the sample continued to live there in 1936. Thirty-eight percent of the 1920 sample moved five or less times, but few displayed the same degree of persistence as Abraham G., a shoemaker, who arrived in Argentina in 1905 and spent the next forty-two years on the 700 block of Calle Pasteur. More typical was Benzion S. who landed in Argentina in 1909, spent ten years living at Dujenes 235, and moved three times in the succeeding three decades.

Thirty six percent of those who joined the Chevrah in 1925 lived in Once; slightly fewer of them lived there in 1936. The decline in mobility from earlier samples is noteworthy: only 17 sample members moved as many as four times. Some 37 percent of those who joined the Chevrah in 1930 lived in Once at the time. Only 24 percent of them lived there in 1945. Only 8 percent of this sample moved as many as four times.

The amount of mobility declines with the 1914–15 sample, while the greatest number of address changes occur among those who figure in the second sample (1905–1910). It is in the second sample, too, that the greatest amount of occupational mobility takes place, suggesting that the 1900s was a unique, formative decade for the Jewish community in Argentina.[48]

Unfortunately, the Chevrah records rarely include the year its members moved. Very partial information indicates that in the early years it was not uncommon for people to move several times within a twelve-month period. The decline of residential mobility suggests that the rent-control law might have contributed to residential stability. It is likely, too, that the Depression had a dampening effect on intra-urban mobility. A third factor, undoubtedly, was the continually worsening housing crisis.

STAGE 4: DISPERSION

In 1936, some 22 percent of the Jewish community resided in Once, while slightly more than a quarter lived in Villa Crespo. That same year, for the first time, a recognizable cluster of Jews appeared in district 18 on the city's north side, which includes the relatively exclusive *barrio* of Palermo (see Figure 3). The census boundary is somewhat misleading, because far more Jews lived in the southern part of the district than in its more exclusive, northern side. Nevertheless, in the next 11 years, the number of Jews in district 5 grew by half, the Jewish population in district 7 grew by about one third, and the Jewish population of district 18 grew by about 5 percent. Meanwhile, Once's Jewish population increased by 10 percent while that of Villa Crespo grew by 67 percent. Thus between 1936 and 1947 the community entered the fourth stage of its history, residential dispersion.

Changes in the community caused by industrialization and by the state's more active participation in the economy contributed to this dispersion. As Jews became more mobile, the traditional rationale for the ghetto became less meaningful. Assimilation, or at least acculturation, reduced the Jews' need for a ghetto. Also as Buenos Aires modernized and acquired cheap rapid transit systems, the distance from residence to workplace became a less compelling variable in deciding where to live. Finally, heightened social consciousness on the part of the central government, resulting in expanded expenditures on social welfare, weakened the community's institutions and reduced the need of Jews to live near them (see Figure 5).

Commercial diffusion closely paralleled the community's residential dispersion. Data from the 1930 sample show that by 1945 slightly more Jews worked dispersed throughout the city than in Once. Between 1927 and 1936, the city periphery, the nonghetto *barrios,* and Buenos Aires province had become significant sources of jobs for Jews. By 1945 Buenos Aires province and the periphery together held as many jobs for Jews as Villa Crespo. This accelerating decentralization coincides with the industrialization of Buenos Aires and with the residential dispersion of the Jewish community between 1936 and 1947. However, the periphery never rivalled Once or Villa Crespo as preferred areas of Jewish settlement.

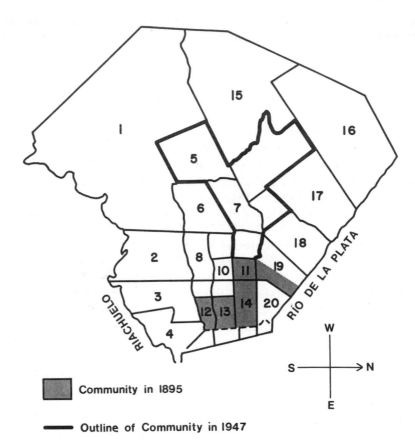

Figure 5. Spatial dispersal of the Jewish community, 1895–1947.

The artisanal form of production limited movement of Jews to the fringes. Those factors that gave the artisan's workshop advantages over the factory—independence, access to family or other cheap but sufficiently experienced labor, low rents, proximity to sources of supply, and nearness to consumers—also influenced residential choice. Only when the factory had marginalized the petty entrepreneur, or when the petty bourgeois had become successful enough to separate his home from his workplace, would the journey to work cease to be an important factor in determining location.

Despite all these changes, in 1947 it was still possible to draw lines around the Jewish community of Buenos Aires with relative ease. The Jewish community remained almost six times as segregated as other immigrant communities. On the basis of the 1936 census, Jews were still 3.5 times as segregated as the city's Italians, 2.7 times as segregated as the Spaniards, 2 times as segregated as the city's French community, and 1.2 times as segregated as the English and Irish. The Jews of the ghettoes, who shared a perception of why they preferred to live together and a common economic reality that strengthened that perception, knew that at least until 1947 "the barrios of Buenos Aires are divided by invisible and insurmountable walls."[49]

Notes

1. On the development of Buenos Aires, *see:* Charles Sargent, *The Spatial Evolution of Greater Buenos Aires* (Tempe: Arizona State University Press, 1974) and James R. Scobie, *Buenos Aires: From Plaza to Suburb, 1870–1910* (New York: Oxford University Press, 1974). See also: James R. Scobie, "Changing Urban Patterns: The Porteño Case, 1880–1910;" Jorge Hardoy and Richard P. Schaedel, eds., *El proceso de urbanización en América desde sus origines hasta neustros dias* (Buenos Aires: 1969), pp. 323–338; and James R. Scobie, "Buenos Aires as a Commercial-Bureaucratic City, 1880–1910," *American Historical Review,* 77, (October 1972), 1034–1073.

2. Thomas A. Turner, *Argentina and the Argentines* (London: S. Sonnenschein and Co., 1892), pp. 13–14 and 16.

3. Pinie Wald, *The Jewish Working Class and Socialist Movement in Argentina* (Buenos Aires: Asociación Mutual Israelita Argentina, 1963), p. 2. In Yiddish. This is the same phenomenon found in New York and London. See: William M. Leiserson, *Adjusting Immigrants and Industry* (New York: Harper & Brothers, 1924), p. 30 and William J. Fishman, *Jewish Radicals* (New York: Pantheon Books, 1974), p. 153.

4. Wald, *The Jewish Working Class,* p. 2 and Bernard D. Ansel, "Discord Among Western and Eastern European Jews in Argentina," *American Jewish Historical Quarterly,* 60, (December 1970), pp. 151–158.

5. Sample data.

6. **Population Densities per Hectare of Selected Districts, 1895–1947**

				YEAR			
District	*1895*	*1904*	*1909*	*1914*	*1924*	*1936*	*1947*
1, 3, 5, 7	247.1						
9	—	227.0	252.0	287.5	328.7	296.6	334.9
11	—	291.0	302.0	339.5	382.8	405.6	499.1
14	—	227.0	208.0	226.6	250.0	271.4	300.3
15	—	5.0	13.0	30.1	42.3	111.8	140.6
Citywide	37.5	55.0	68.0	88.0	97.0	129.8	160.5

Source: National and Municipal censuses.
Ciudad de Buenos Aires, Intendencia Municipal, *Proyecto orgánico para la urbanización del municipio* (Buenos Aires: Talleres Peuser, 1925), p. 76.

7. Sample data.

8. On changing styles in *porteño* architecture in the nineteenth century *see:* Diana Hernando, "Casa y familia," (Los Angeles: unpublished doctoral dissertation, UCLA, 1973). The manuscript census of 1895 revealed that enumerators were less than completely thorough in describing housing conditions. Partial data indicate that the majority of Jews lived in brick buildings. Slightly more than 75 percent for whom there are data lived in one-story buildings, about 20 percent lived in two-story buildings, while the rest lived in three-story buildings, basements or conventillos. Sample data. Scobie indicates that living conditions did not determine a building's classification as a conventillo. Rather, in order to be considered a tenement a building must have had at least 30 tenants. *See* Scobie, *Buenos Aires,* p. 147.

9. Comisión Directiva del Censo, *Segundo censo,* vol. 3 p. xx. *See* Oscar Yujnovsky's excellent article "Políticas de vivienda en la Ciudad de Buenos Aires (1880–1914)," *Desarollo Economico,* 14, (1974), p. 334.

10. The data come from Scobie, *Buenos Aires,* p. 272. The memories of 1871 remained strong. In 1919, for example, the municipality turned its attention to the regulation of sanitary conditions in pawn shops. All goods had to be disinfected prior to sale. Nor could pawn shops be located near food depots, food processing establishments, or lodgings. A series of other measures to promote cleanliness were also promulgated. These were extensions of 1886 legislation that ordered all contaminated clothing and furniture burned. *See:* Municipalidad de Buenos Aires, *Digesto Municipal, 1936* (Buenos Aires: Municipalidad de Buenos Aires, 1936), p. 880.

11. Sargent, *The Spatial Evolution,* p. 24.

12. Mario Bravo, *La ciudad libre,* quoted in Oscar Yujnovsky, "Políticas de vivienda en la ciudad de Buenos Aires (1880–1914)," *Desarollo Economico,* 14, n. 7–9 (1974), p. 372.

13. Louis Wirth, "The Ghetto," Albert J. Reiss, ed., *Louis Wirth on Cities and Social Life* (Chicago: University of Chicago Press, 1964), p. 84. This article is a distillation of Wirth's classic study, *The Ghetto* (Chicago: University of Chicago Press, 1928).

14. Wirth, "The Ghetto," pp. 90–92.

15. Israel Cohen, *Jewish Life in Modern Times* (New York: Dodd, Mead & Co., 1929) 2nd edition, quoted in Wirth, "The Ghetto," p. 92.

16. Nicolás Rapoport, "Breve historia del hospital," Nicolás Rapoport, ed., *Libro del cincuentenario de la Ezrah y Hospital Israelita* (Buenos Aires: Talleres Graficos Julio Kaufman, 1950), p. 29.

17. On the role of the Anglo-Jewish community in London's Jewish community, *see:* A. M. Hyamson, *A History of the Jews in England* (London: Chattas and Windar, 1908) and V. D. Lipman, *A Century of Social Service, 1859–1959* (London: Routledge and Kegan Paul, 1959).

18. Arthur A. Goren, *New York Jews and the Quest for Community* (New York: Columbia University Press, 1970), p. 248.

19. On secularism among the immigrants, see: Haim Avni, "Argentine Jewry," Part III, *Dispersion and Unity,* 15–16 (1972), 159.

20. *See: El Industrial Maderero,* V, 44 (July 1944) 47–54.

21. *Juventud,* 1 (1911), 10.

22. Use of one or another segregation index has been employed most often to determine

the degree of black segregation in United States cities. For a discussion of the literature on residential segregation, *see:* Karl E. Taeuber and Alma F. Taeuber, *Negroes in Cities* (New York: Atheneum, 1972), pp. 14–25. The index of dissimilarity is computed in the following way:

1. Compute:

$$\frac{\text{Jews}}{\text{non-Jews (population minus Jews)}} = \text{citywide percentage for the city as a whole.}$$

2. Compute:

$$\frac{\text{Jews}}{\text{non-Jews}} \text{ for each district.}$$

3. Select those districts where $\frac{\text{Jews}}{\text{non-Jews}}$ is greater than for the city as a whole.

4. Add the number of Jews in these districts. Add the number of non-Jews in these districts.

5. Compute:

$$\frac{\text{Jews in districts}}{\text{Jews in the city}} \text{ minus } \frac{\text{non-Jews in districts}}{\text{non-Jews in the city}} \times 100 = \text{INDEX}$$

Index of Dissimilarity, Buenos Aires, 1895–1947

Year	Jews	80% East[1] European	Foreigners[2]	Italians	Spaniards	French	English
1895	57.8	50.6	8.9	12.1	23.5	19.4	27.8
1904	45.9	n.d.	10.0	n.d.	n.d.	n.d.	n.d.
1909	47.5	48.2	8.1	12.0	21.2	19.3	27.6
1914	n.d.	38.7	10.1	11.2	18.7	19.7	28.9
1936	40.3	29.4	6.5	11.6	14.9	21.2	33.4[3]
1947	32.6	n.d.	5.7	n.d.	n.d.	n.d.	n.d.

[1] This column is an attempt to control for the presence of western Europeans in the first column. The possibility remains that the percentage for 1936 should be higher to reflect the increased Polish immigration of the early 1930s.

Eastern European includes: Russians, Poles, Rumanians, and Lithuanians.

[2] Includes eastern Europeans.

[3] Includes both English and Irish.

Sources: 1895 Census, vol. 2, pp. 15, 36; 1904 Census, 3–5, p. 70; 1909 Census, vol. 1, pp. 3–17, 88–93; 1914 Census, vol. 4, pp. 129–150; 1936 Census, vol. 2, pp. 130–171, vol. 3, pp. 254–292; 1947 Census, vol. 1, pp. 50–60.

23. An 1890 survey of New York's Lower East Side indicated that 56 percent of the city's Jews lived in the three wards that comprised the neighborhood. Densities ranged between 289.7 and 523.6 people per acre. By 1910, the 10th ward, with more than 700 people per acre, was the densest in the city. *See:* Moses Rischin, *The Promised City* (New York: Harper & Row, 1962), pp. 79–80 and Elias Tcherikower, ed., *The Early Jewish Labor Movement in the United States* (New York: YIVO, 1961), p. 154. London's East End also followed a classic pattern of ghettoization and overcrowding. As the center city expanded administratively and commercially, ghetto dwellings were demolished, thus increasing densities. *See:* Lloyd P. Gartner,

The Jewish Immigrant in England, 1870–1914 (London: George Allen & Unwin, Ltd., 1960), p. 147.

24. *See* table: footnote 6.

25. James R. Scobie, *Buenos Aires,* 261.

26. Cuidad de Buenos Aires, *Censo general de población, edificación, comercio e industrias, 1904* (Buenos Aires: Compañia Sud-americano de Billetes de Banco, 1906), p. 121.

27. Ciudad de Buenos Aires, *Censo general de 1909,* 1.3 (Buenos Aires: Compañia Sud-americano de Billetes de Banco, 1910), 1, pp. ix–x.

28. Buenos Aires, *Censo . . . 1909,* 1 pp. 177–179. By 1909, there were 5,463, 2,933, and 4,288 buildings in districts 9, 11, and 14 respectively. Eighty-five percent of the structures in district 9 were one-story high, 63 percent of those in district 11 were one-story tall, while only half of those in district 14 were one-floor tall. Only district 14 contained more than 100 buildings three or more floors high. Buenos Aires, *Censo . . . 1909,* 1 pp. 167–170.

29. República Argentina, Departamento Nacional del Trabajo, *Boletín,* vol. 5 (June 1908), p. 234.

30. United States, Department of Commerce, *Wearing Apparel in Argentina* (Washington: *Government Printing Office,* 1918), p. 47.

31. Roger Babson, *The Future of South America* (Boston: Little, Brown & Co., 1916), p. 227.

32. Alejandro E. Bunge, *Los problemas económicos del presente* (Buenos Aires: n.p., 1920), p. 157.

33. United States, Bureau of Labor Statistics, *Monthly Labor Review* (December 1921), 76; and (May 1931), 210.

34. United States, Bureau of Labor Statistics, *Monthly Labor Review* (June 1920), 81.

35. United States. Bureau of Labor Statistics. *Monthly Labor Review* (December 1921), 161; (February 1922), 137–138; (October 1922), 185; (October 1923), 115; and (April 1925), 171.

36. United States, Bureau of Labor Statistics, *Monthly Labor Review* (June 1920), 81.

37. United States, Department of Commerce, *Shoe and Leather Trade in Argentina, Chile, Peru, and Uruguay* (Washington: Government Printing Office, 1910), p. 24.

38. Dickmann, quoted in Yujnovsky, "Politicas," p. 337.

39. In the 1880s, Municipal Intendent Torcuato de Alvear oversaw the construction of a few units in which to house city employees. In 1899, the Buenos Aires and Southern Railway built 52 houses in Banfield, a Buenos Aires suburb, for its employees. Six years later, the municipality built some 70 units but took no further action on a proposed working-class suburb of 30,000 people. In 1907, a wealthy *porteño* left the city funds to be used to construct workers' housing. The *barrio* Buteler, named in the donor's honor, was administered by the *Patronato del Obrero* (Workers' Charity), a society of upper-class women, not by the city. Four years later, the Jockey Club, the most elite of Buenos Aires' clubs, donated 50 million pesos to construct inexpensive housing in the city. Within a year 65 units had been completed and 116 more were under construction. Obviously, the amount of construction was insufficient for its purpose.

40. United States, Bureau of Labor Statistics, *Monthly Labor Review* (June 1920), 80–81.

41. In 1909, 49 percent of the buildings in Buenos Aires housed families only, 17 percent families and businesses, and six percent workshops and businesses. Single family housing accounted for 28 percent of all construction. Forty-four percent of the structures in district 9 housed families, 26 percent families and businesses, and eight percent workshops and businesses. Less than 25 percent were single family units. Some 43 percent of the housing stock in district 11 was inhabited by families, 34 percent by families and businesses, four percent by businesses and workshops, and 18 percent were single family dwellings. One-third of the buildings in district 14 were inhabited by families, 16 percent by families and businesses, and 11 percent were privately owned homes. Buenos Aires, *Censo . . . 1909*, 1 p. 179.

42. David Ward, "The Emergence of Central Immigrant Ghettoes in American Cities: 1840–1920," ed. Larry S. Bourne, *Internal Structure of the City* (New York: Oxford University Press, 1971), pp. 294–296.

43. Business addresses were compared to residence addresses to determine: (a) whether the two were the same, (b) whether they were on the same block, (c) whether they were more than a horizontal block apart, and (d) whether business and residence fell in the same district. The data suggest the importance of the workplace in determining housing location.

44. Sample data.

45. Sample data.

46. *Enciclopedia Judaica Castellana* (Mexico: *Editorial Enciclopedia Judaica Castellana*, 1948), vol. 2, p. 411.

47. On *barrio* Once in the nineteenth century, *see:* Municipalidad de la ciudad de Buenos Aires, *Evolución urbana de la ciudad de Buenos Aires* (Buenos Aires: Municipalidad de la Ciudad de Buenos Aires, 1972).

48. Sample data.

49. Estela Canto, *El ratrato y la imagen* (Buenos Aires: Editorial Losada, 1950), p. 119.

CHAPTER 5

WORK AND MOBILITY

Opportunities for upward occupational mobility are obviously defined and limited by the prevailing political and economic climate. For almost the entire first half of the twentieth century, genuine prosperity in Argentina depended on the success of the agro-export sector; its performance fluctuating wildly from year to year. The occupational shifts of the Jewish community in Buenos Aires offer valuable insights into the effects of these chronic structural problems in the economy on social mobility and community cohesion.

The study of occupational structure—what happens to entire occupational groups—and of occupational mobility—what happens to individual workers—helps to clarify the nature of Argentina's occupational universe and how it changed with industrialization and urbanization. Occupational mobility, which occurs within the more comprehensive occupational structure, can be upward, downward, lateral, or it may not occur at all. Furthermore, mobility need not be unilinear. Jews in Buenos Aires, for instance, often evidenced a pattern of "inconsistency" as individuals rose on the occupational ladder only to fall back into the category from which they came.[1]

The sample data in this chapter are derived from the records of the 1895 Argentine census manuscript for Buenos Aires, from the membership applications and rolls of the Chevrah Keduscha and of more than 100 other voluntary and civic associations, from city directories, from community almanacs, and from telephone books for the city of Buenos Aires. The occupational history of the 1,500 sample members was traced from the year each joined the Chevrah as far as possible toward the present. Records, however, rarely conform to the needs of historians, and over the course of four decades many people disappeared from the membership rolls. Why they left the Chevrah can be surmised; how much they differed from those who remained is more difficult to discern. In all cases, description is limited to those who could be traced successfully.

TECHNOLOGICAL CHANGE

Argentina's transition to a mass society was rocky, characterized by upheaval and unrest. Technological change, imported from Europe and the United States, resulted in important alterations in the work of almost all trades. In some cases technology was a boon, easing the strain of physical labor, simplifying productive processes, and allowing for higher wages. In other instances, technological innovation wrought havoc on working-class life. Sometimes the two processes occurred simultaneously. Where technology could be turned to their advantage, Jews remained in the trades; where it proved injurious, they sought other means of livelihood.

Workers often found it difficult, if not impossible, to adjust to new techniques of production. In such cases the confrontation between the worker and the machine had serious consequences. In his classic study of the English working class, historian E. P. Thompson noted that "even where an old skill was replaced by a new process requiring equal or greater skill, we rarely find the same workers transferred from one to the other, or from domestic to factory production."[1a] The marginalization that Thompson describes is called displacement of skill; it is "the loss of opportunity to sell acquired skill at the rate of remuneration which would have been received if the machinery had not been introduced."[2] The effects of skill displacement depend on the speed with which the machine is introduced, the mobility of the affected workers, the machine's success in cutting prices and increasing demand, how many workers are displaced, and whether the affected worker can participate in the new process. Historically, "the initial blow of the new process is likely to fall most heavily on skilled workmen."[3]

Machinery not only reduces the amount of labor involved but changes the type of labor needed. Skill displacement invariably produces marked changes in the occupational structure and affects the degree of occupational mobility in a society. As industrialization gripped Argentina in the nineteenth and twentieth centuries, the resultant displacement of skill left the typical Argentine artisan with four options. Mechanization of his trade could result in unemployment; he could seek employment as a factory worker, which would require less or different kinds of skill and might pay less; he could continue to produce in traditional ways, competing at a disadvantage in a changing market and becoming increasingly marginalized; or he could attempt to accumulate sufficient capital to become an entrepreneur.[4]

As long as other avenues of employment remained open, Jews tended not to enter factories. Sample data indicate that Jews preferred to work for others in small workshops, to become independent petty producers, or to take up occupations like street vending that disguised their underemployment. One student of Jewish labor in the United States noted that the Jewish wage worker was ". . . strongly motivated to become a tradesman; the artisan to concentrate on the commercial aspects of his occupation."[5] The same pattern held true in Argentina. Thus the marginal producer and the aspiring entrepreneur are more important in the Argentine case then the factory worker or the unemployed.

Even if he tried to escape the trend toward mechanization, the artisan was subject to unemployment. Marco-economic phenomena—depression, recession, industrialization—and the very nature of the trades enforced idleness. Most skilled trades were seasonal. Only the unskilled could shift from one industry, or job, to another.[6] According to the United States Department of Commerce, "there is a great deal of unemployment in Buenos Aires at certain times of the year. . . . Skilled labor for industrial work is not abundant though at times this type of labor is often found unemployed."[7]

THE EARLY IMMIGRANTS

Russian Jewish immigrants to Argentina soon learned that wealth, status, and land ownership were intimately related. Those Jews who entered the country under the auspices of the Jewish Colonization Association could hope to become small landowners after they fulfilled the terms of their contracts, but the vast majority, cut off from access to the land, sought other paths to economic security. The range of opportunities open to these immigrants was limited. Native Argentines or other immigrants, most from Spain or Italy, already filled established positions. Training, lack of prior experience, cultural prediliction, and the inability to accumulate capital constrained Jews from moving into the sectors of the economy that were demonstrating dynamism at the turn of the century.

The realities of the Argentine economy, coupled with the training and experience that Jews had acquired in eastern Europe, combined to foster the working-class and petty bourgeois activities of the immi-

grants. In 1909, Samuel Halphon, an emissary of the Jewish Colonization Association, reported that "our co-religionists in Argentina
include a large number of trades and they may be classified by
branches, according to their countries or origin. The Russians are generally engaged in the furniture trade, the Turks—in habadashery, the
Moroccans—in cloth and ready made clothing, the French, Germans,
Dutch, etc.,—in jewelry. Some of them are extremely rich but most of
them are only small tradesmen. The number of Jews in this country
include a certain number of clerks and members of the liberal professions. Finally, the Russian Jews include a very large number of workers employed in all types of manual labor," including the garment
industry. Halphon discovered only 100 Jewish professionals in the
entire country.[8]

The presence of a large working class imbued the Jewish community with a pluralistic flavor. No fewer than 36 percent of those in any
sample who had an occupation were workers, a percentage that rises
significantly if the unemployed and miscellaneously occupied are
added to the working class. In all cases, those possessing a degree of

**Table 5-1.   Occupations of Sample Members at Time of Membership in the
Chevrah, 1895–1930[1]**

Classification	1895[1]	1905	1915	1920	1925	1930
Unskilled and menial service	14	—	8	7	5	3
Semiskilled and service	19	8	16	11	30	32
Rural semiskilled and service	4	—	—	6	—	—
Skilled	101	50	86	147	122	98
Low nonmanual	20	14	16	31	66	74
Middle and unspecified nonmanual	66	81	71	68	33	51
High nonmanual	4	1	3	2	4	3
Low professional	4	5	3	4	9	8
High professional	3	2	2	2	4	7
Miscellaneous and unknown	68	117	73	—	5	2
Totals						
Workers	138	58	110	171	157	133
Nonmanual	90	96	90	101	103	128
Professional	7	7	5	6	13	15
Miscellaneous	68	117	73	—	5	2

Notes: [1]For a complete discussion of the occupational classification system used, see:
Mark D. Szuchman and Eugene F. Sofer, "The State of Occupational
Stratification Studies in Argentina: A Classificatory Scheme," *Latin American
Research Review*, XI:1 (Spring 1976), 159–172.
[2]N = 303 and is equal to the number of males enumerated in the 1895 census.
In samples 2 through 6, n = 278.

Source: Sample data.

Table 5-2. Occupational Mobility of Members in Sample 1[1]

	OCCUPATIONAL CHANGE				
Classification[2]	No change	Upward	Downward	Inconsistent	Membership occ. = death occ.[3]
Workers (#)	8	12	—	10	18
(%)	27	40	—	33	60
Nonmanual (#)	4	1	6	2[4]	6
(%)	31	8	46	15	46

Notes: [1]$N = 43$; untraceables $= 90$, all of whom either moved or dropped out of the Chevrah.
[2]Does not include one professional who remained a professional until his death.
[3]Includes those whose occupation at death was the same as their occupation at membership in spite of the change in 1927.
[4]Of the two nonmanual inconsistents, one was upwardly mobile, the other downwardly mobile.

Source: Sample data.

skill far outnumbered their semiskilled or unskilled compatriots. As late as 1930, close to half of those who joined the Chevrah were workers (see Table 5-1).

The experiences of the 1,500 sample members reflect the difficulties Jewish workers typically encountered in the Argentine capital. Tables 5-2–5-7 indicate that in spite of occasionally significant but often temporary upward mobility, increasingly high percentages of those who joined the Chevrah as workers died as workers. Only those who joined between 1905 and 1910 experienced a different pattern. Thus, the mobility that eastern European Jews experienced and the community's occupational structure were quite fragile. Over the first

Table 5-3. Occupational Mobility of Sample 2 Members (1905–10)[1]

	OCCUPATIONAL CHANGE				
Classification	No change	Upward	Downward	Inconsistent	Membership occ. = death occ.
Workers (#)	21	55	—	3	24
(%)	27	70		3	30
Nonmanual (#)	26	—	35	2[2]	28
(%)	41	—	56	3	44
Professional (#)	1	—	4	1	2
(%)	16	—	67	16	33

Notes: [1]$N = 148$; untraceables $= 130$, four of whom were still alive in 1973 and 57 of whom moved or dropped out of the Chevrah.
[2]The two nonmanual inconsistents were both downwardly mobile.

Source: Sample data.

Table 5-4.   Occupational Mobility of Sample 3 Members (1914–15)[1]

		OCCUPATIONAL CHANGE			
Classification	No change	Upward	Downward	Inconsistent	Membership occ. = death occ.
Workers (#)	22	14	—	16	38
(%)	42	27	—	31	73
Nonmanual (#)	25	—	18	3[2]	28
(%)	54	—	39	7	61
Professional (#)	3	—	—	—	3
(%)	100	—	—	—	100

Notes: [1]N = 101; untraceable = 167, ten of whom were still alive in 1973 and 46 of whom moved or dropped out of the Chevrah.
[2]The three nonmanual inconsistents were all downwardly mobile.

Source: Sample data.

half century of Jewish life in Buenos Aires, most workers experienced mobility only fleetingly, if at all. Most of the mobility that did occur was the result of some Jews perceiving new possibilities and new markets. But even these innovators experienced difficulties. One third of those who were able temporarily to leave the working class slid back into it, and even those owners who began as owners had to contend with the distinct possibility of downward mobility. I have called this phenomenon "inconsistent" mobility.

José Luis R. was typical of those who remained in the working class. A 31-year-old watchmaker when he was enumerated in the 1895 census, he stayed at this craft until his death in 1925 at age 62. His entire estate consisted of old clothes and ten watches. Abram S., who

Table 5-5.   Occupational Mobility of Sample 4 Members (1920)[1]

		OCCUPATIONAL CHANGE			
Classification	No change	Upward	Downward	Inconsistent	Membership occ. = death occ.
Workers (#)	17	10	—	13	30
(%)	43	25	—	32	75
Nonmanual (#)	21	—	18	2[2]	23
(%)	51	—	44	5	56
Professional (#)	2	—	—	1	3
(%)	67	—	—	33	100

Notes: [1]N = 84; untraceables = 194, nine of whom were still alive in 1973 and 66 of whom moved or dropped out of the Chevrah.
[2]Of the two nonmanual inconsistents, one was upwardly mobile, the other downwardly mobile.

Source: Sample data.

Table 5-6. Occupational Mobility of Sample 5 Members (1925)[1]

| Classification | OCCUPATIONAL CHANGE | | | | |
	No change	Upward	Downward	Inconsistent	Membership occ. = death occ.
Workers (#)	16	2	—	9	25
(%)	59	7	—	34	94
Nonmanual (#)	7	1	18[2]	—	7
(%)	27	4	69	—	27
Professional (#)	3	—	—	—	3
(%)	100	—	—	—	100

Notes: [1]N = 56; untraceable = 222, 64 of whom were still alive in 1973 and 48 of whom moved or dropped out of the Chevrah.
[2]Only one of the inconsistents was upwardly mobile, rising to the professional category but dying a worker.

Source: Sample data.

joined the Chevrah in 1910, represents a variation of this same pattern. A tailor in 1895, he undertook a lateral job shift and became a butcher. He, too, spent his entire life in the working class. On the other hand, Isaac C. entered Argentina at age 23, married and the father of a five-month-old daughter. Literate, but lacking formal education, he worked as a hatmaker. When he joined the Chevrah ten years later, he listed his occupation as businessman, having accumulated sufficient capital to open a small hat and cap factory. Nevertheless, fully 60 percent of those Jews in the 1895 sample who could be traced died as workers, much as they had begun.

This first generation included a large number of remarkable men and women who helped to found and eventually led many of the community's voluntary and commercial associations. Soly Borok, a foun-

Table 5-7. Occupational Mobility of Sample 6 Members (1930)[1]

| Classification | OCCUPATIONAL CHANGE | | | | |
	No change	Upward	Downward	Inconsistent	Membership occ. = death occ.
Workers (#)	18	5	—	3	21
(%)	69	19	—	12	81
Nonmanual (#)	15	—	12	—	15
(%)	56	—	44	—	56
Professional (#)	4	—	2	—	4
(%)	67	—	33	—	67

Notes: [1]N = 59; untraceable = 219, 81 of whom were still alive in 1973 and 56 of whom moved or dropped out of the Chevrah.

Source: Sample data.

der of the Chevrah and president of the Unión Israelita, was sufficiently well-off to contribute funds to the Anglo-Jewish Association in London. Solomon Liebeschutz, also financially secure, served as president of the Chevrah in 1906, helped to establish both the Jewish Committee to Honor the Argentine Centenary and the Committee to Aid Victims of the Morrocan War (1912), and served as the community's rabbi as well.

Among those who joined the Chevrah between 1905 and 1910, more than half of the traceable members employed in nonmanual occupations had undergone downward mobility by 1927. For a variety of reasons, this phenomenon escaped the attention of relevant Argentine authorities. The Argentine Department of Labor excluded from its investigations "the self-employed artisan who works in his home with one or several workers, because his work differs so from the homework that is genuinely ours that it cannot be considered the subject of the same study or regulation. It is more correctly 'petty industry' which must include all homes, workshops, and factories which employ from one to five workers in the service of someone self-employed."[9] Elsewhere, the Labor Department offered some insight into both the difficulties of regulating such work and the exploitation inherent in it. Home work in Argentina, it noted, was "as anonymous here as abroad. The employer always finds someone to give work to and the workers who suffer his impositions can do nothing. The workers are always able to deliver the work to third parties and neither the employer nor the authorities can prevent it."[10] Jewish workers and their mostly Jewish employers suffered both from profound economic insecurity and from exploitation reminiscent of their situation in Russia. Although the number of Jewish businesses expanded during the 1920s, there is no evidence that the government tried to slow the downward mobility of nonmanual workers which characterized the Jewish community's occupational structure. The expansion of the commercial and service sectors was not marked by a concurrent increase in the economic security of their members.

The effects of Argentina's industralization on the Jewish community as the twentieth century progressed can be seen in an examination of the occupations of the sons and sons-in-law of sample members (Table 5-8). Most clearly, the working-class component of the community declined to about one-third. At the same time, however, the percentage of skilled workers declined from an adjusted low of 38 percent to only 17 percent. This was accompanied by a rise in both the unskilled and semiskilled categories, reflecting the tendency of labor to lose skills during industrialization. It seems clear, too, that would-be

TABLE 5-8.   Occupations of Surviving Sons and Sons-in-law (1949–1973)[1]

Classification	Total	AMIA Members[2]	non-AMIA members
Unskilled and menial service	61	39	22
Semiskilled and service	137	77	60
Rural semiskilled and service	4	2	2
Skilled	213	125	88
Low nonmanual	362	229	133
Middle and unspecified nonmanual	231	136	95
High nonmanual	19	11	8
Low professional	43	18	25
High profesional	134	91	43
Miscellaneous and unknown	65	41	24
Totals			
Workers	415 (33%)	233 (33%)	172 (34%)
Nonmanual	612 (48%)	376 (49%)	236 (47%)
Professional	177 (14%)	109 (14%)	68 (14%)
Miscellaneous	65 (5%)	41 (4%)	24 (5%)
	1269	769	500

Notes: [1]$N = 1269$; [2]The Chevrah changed its name to the AMIA in 1941.
Source: Sample data.

skilled workers were faced with the choice of the factory or self-employment.

Overall among all the samples, the highest percentages of up-wardly mobile workers are found, not coincidentally, in the first two samples. These immigrants arrived during an era of expansion and they could identify economic opportunities and take advantage of them. Competition remained surmountable. The first Jews soon dominated certain businesses and trades, like hat and capmaking. That dominance meant economic gain for some, but whatever advantages accrued to the first wave of immigrants disappeared as class lines began to harden.

THE GARMENT INDUSTRY

In the first years of the twentieth century, the garment industry attracted more Jewish workers than any other, and the vast majority of those who began life as garment workers died that way. The number of those who became owners of garment-related firms, as well as those who began as owners, declined consistently between 1895 and 1930. In the 1920 and 1925 samples, some of those who had been garment workers appeared in other occupations, suggesting that the industry was suffering, that it was less likely to attract Jewish newcomers, and that the level of skill required to work in the needle trades had declined to the point where workers felt they could shift into other occupations without losing the benefit of a lifetime's experience.

Mass production of clothing was less than four decades old in 1900 but had made great strides since the U.S. Civil War. The invention of the sewing machine in 1846, the development of cutting and pressing machines, and subsequent modifications and improvements in all three, combined with the realization that most men had similar body types and that garments could be manufactured to fit a type rather than an individual, spurred mass production.[11] The well-to-do continued to be clothed by custom tailors, but the poor and middle class could now purchase ready-made, mass-produced clothing instead of wearing homemade or second-hand garments.

Such clothing made sense. It was more convenient for the worker or farm laborer to buy a ready-made suit than to save for a custom-made one. Before World War I, a ready-made suit cost between 30 and 35 pesos, or about 13 dollars; custom-made garments sold for between 30 and 35 dollars. Wartime inflation caused a 30 percent increase in prices and a 50 percent drop in consumption. Unavoidable production costs kept even the price of ready-made clothing high.[12] Nevertheless, by World War I, the ready-made suit had replaced refurbished old clothes in popular preference, even though clothing still absorbed a significant portion of the working-class budget.

The traditional needle trades—the men's, women's, and children's clothing industries, the millinery, cloth hat, and cap industries, and the fur trades—had started to change even before the era of mass Jewish immigration. To these trades Jews introduced the task system. A team of tailors, each with a specific function, combined to produce an entire garment. Theoretically, the more hours they worked, the more garments they made, and the more they were paid. In reality, in John R. Commons' phrase, the Jewish system was "perhaps the most ingenius and effective means of over-exertion known to modern industry."[13]

As the resistance of Argentine consumers to mass-produced clothing weakened at the end of the nineteenth century, Jewish tailors, relying on machines and the extreme subdivision of labor that characterized workshop production, marginalized the more traditional custom tailors. The Argentine Department of Labor, in a study of the task system, identified thirteen different categories of garment workers in the ready-made clothing industry.[14] As each task became more well-defined, tailors needed less skill. The garment industry became the employer of women, children, semiskilled workers, and unemployed intellectuals with no skills at all. Many *luftmenschen* [a Yiddish phrase describing people with no fixed occupation] gravitated to the industry.

Most of the ready-made clothing for sale in Buenos Aires was the result of piecework. As late as 1918, not a single Argentine factory devoted itself to producing ready-made clothing, in spite of the fact that throughout the country about half of all clothing purchased was mass produced.

In 1914, there were some 4,000 firms, worth about $20 million, that manufactured clothing in Argentina. Of them, the United States Department of Commerce reported:

> This large number of firms engaged in the manufacture of apparel does not give a true idea of the importance of this industry. By far the largest part are small custom tailors, private dressmakers, etc., and industries of the small workshop or sweatshop type, which buy their raw materials from the wholesaler or even from the retailer, according to the importance of their trade. In general it may be said that there are about 60 firms that merit the title cutters up.[15]

By 1910, Jewish clothing firms did an estimated six million pesos worth of business and employed, including women and children, some 600 workers.[16] The vast majority were pieceworkers who earned about 70 pesos a month; children, who performed the same work as adults, earned between 6 and 10 pesos a month. The average workday was ten to fourteen hours long.

Most work was performed for contractors. For instance, the largest commercial houses, department stores like Harrod's and Gath y Chaves, employed "fifty or more women charged with carrying work home for 300 or more workers. Each of them is thus converted into the chief of a small workshop in which the workers are charged with the manufacture while they must receive and deliver the article. The house pays for the article at a pre-arranged price, but in the majority of cases the payment which reaches the workers is considerably reduced."[17] Homeworkers, the first time they worked for a particular house, also had to leave a deposit equal to the value of the merchandise they were taking.

As soon as several tailors began to share responsibility for a garment, the industry became exploitative. The evils of the contracting system, especially the sweatshop, accompanied mass production and horrified workers and social critics alike.[18] Such evils stemmed from the nature of the system itself; as Sidney and Beatrice Webb, the Fabian Socialists, remarked about the industry in London, "wholesale distribution necessitate[d] wholesale production."[19]

Rapidity of production was of the highest priority for manufacturers because the seasonal nature of the industry and almost constant fluctuations in fashion required flexibility. In this respect, the small operator had certain advantages over the factory. Foot-powered sewing machines, low rental costs, and cheap labor made twelve to eighteen hour days possible. Often, needle-trades workers owned their own sewing machines, further reducing the manufacturer's production costs.

Perhaps no single feature facilitated the spread of the sweating system as much as the sewing machine. The Singer Company introduced its first machines to Argentina in 1876 for sale on consignment and thirty years later opened its own offices in Buenos Aires. Singer sold, serviced, and exhibited its own product so extensively that eventually the company owned more than 300 outlets in Argentina.[20] The sewing machine's wide availability helped spread the sweatshop through the working-class neighborhoods of Buenos Aires. It provided workers with a source of savings; in times of extreme need they could pawn their machines. Because of its low cost, the sewing machine was also a favored form of work-stimulating charity in the Jewish community.

Jews took their techniques of production, none of them more infamous than sweating, with them wherever they settled. The Webbs' definition of sweating—"unusually low rates of wages, excessive hours of labour, and unsanitary workplaces" does not convey the horrors of a system so execrable that it attracted the attention of such diverse social observers as the British House of Lords, U.S. urban reformer Jacob Riis, and the *porteño* working-class newspaper *El Obrero*.[21] There can be no doubt that sweatshops were common to petty production in Buenos Aires. In 1891, *El Obrero* defined the system this way:

> A contractor arranges the price of work with the capitalist and carries it to his home. He immediately gives the piece work to the workers who come to work in his house. The house is called a sweatshop, the workers the sweated, because to earn a scarcely acceptable salary they must work until they sweat in torrents. The contractor is the master sweater.

The newspaper complained that "the large tailor shops, shoemaking shops, millinery businesses, etc., in Buenos Aires all earn abundant percentages through this infamous system that kills men and women in a short time, or at least quickly ruins their health."[22] During the slack season, even first-class tailors became pieceworkers for the ready-made clothing houses, despite receiving far less than their customary wages.

The sweating system provided *porteño* manufacturers with the same benefits experienced by their counterparts in other countries. Certain tasks in the clothing, shoemaking, and textile industries could be performed easily in the home. The manufacturers enjoyed important economics of rent, labor, and machinery while piecework offered them a ready pool of sufficiently skilled labor at lower wages. For instance, tailors in first-class establishments worked eight or ten hours day and earned between 100 and 120 pesos a month. Pieceworkers took two-and-a-half, fourteen-hour days to make a coat for which they received between 10 and 12 pesos. According to working-class militant Adrián Patroni, "working continuously (something that doesn't happen . . . because of the plethora of unemployed workers) [pieceworkers] can produce about 10 coats a month, whose total price is from 100 to 120 pesos. At first glance it seems that they had earned the same salary as the master who works eight or ten hours in the shop. In reality, [the pieceworker] not only works four or five more hours a day but must subtract from the 100 or 120 pesos what he invested in yarn, silk, cotton, coal, kerosene, and rent (because he needs a room that has a lot of light), not counting the value of the machine, irons, table, etc., that he needs. If all this is subtracted, the result, in general, will be that he earns only 70 to 90 pesos a month."[23]

The contractor, a middleman between the manufacturer and the pieceworker, was at the center of the "Jewish" system of production. Like those he employed, the Jewish contractor was himself a tailor, but he was also an organizer of work. John R. Commons' classic description of the New York contractor also holds true for Buenos Aires:

> . . . [the contractor is] largely responsible for the primitive mode of production,—for the foot power sewing machine, for the shops in the alleys, in the attics, on top floors, above stables, and in some cases in the homes of the people.
> . . . As there is no investment in goods, the contractor runs no risk. Little managing ability is required, because the number of employees is small.
> . . . The contractor himself works unlimited hours. . . . He holds his own mainly because of his ability to get cheap labor, and is in reality merely the agent of the manufacturer for that purpose. In this he generally succeeds, because he lives among the poorest class of people, knows

them personally, and knowing their circumstances can drive the hardest kind of bargain.[24]

During the busy season, the contractor could accumulate capital, but the exigencies of the industry usually prevented any meaningful savings. The better part of the year was marked by cutthroat competition and meager profits. In the ready-made clothing industry, only the manufacturer made money. There was even enough validity to the contractors' claims that they shared the workers' interests to prompt early garment workers unions in Buenos Aires to accept contractors as members.[25]

The records of the Chevrah suggest that with 100 pesos, a garment worker could become a boss. This contributed to a proliferation of both contractors and shops.[26] As the number of contractors increased, the size of the shop decreased. Contractors frequently alternated between being workers and employers, and they benefited from large pools of available labor, much of it women workers.

At the manufacturing level, local manufacturers shared control of the Argentine garments industry with wholesale importers, retail importers, and foreign-owned companies. The larger establishments either supported their own workshops or bought directly from smaller manufacturers, thus eliminating the wholesaler. Petty proprietors who successfully accumulated a few hundred pesos, or credit for that amount, also tried to deal directly with retailers. Such small operators needed longer-term credit than their larger competitors because "with the limited capital with which they operate it is necessary for them to dispose of the goods and collect for them before they can square their accounts."[27]

Foreign competition was always an important factor. It was in the cheaper lines that the domestic industry was best able to withstand imports. Inexpensively produced shirts, ties, hats, and caps dominated their respective markets because tariffs were sufficiently high to prevent imports from underselling domestic products.

Until Argentine industry, especially textiles, experienced its period of growth in the 1930s, foreign goods dominated the more expensive, better quality market. Also, the primitive state of the pre-World War I Argentine textile industry meant that Argentine clothing workers almost invariably worked with foreign fabrics. Wholesalers, the vast majority of them located in Buenos Aires, handled most of these imports. The bulk of the international trade was concentrated in the hands of about forty large concerns, each capitalized at between

100,000 dollars and 1 million dollars, with access to liberal credit in Argentina and abroad. Few Jews figured in the wholesale end of the business, where Spanish, Italian, and, to a lesser degree, French, English, and German houses predominated. In 1914, only 10 percent of the 370 firms active in textiles were wholly Argentine owned, whereas 24 were of mixed foreign and Argentine ownership.

Those eastern European Jews who did work as wholesalers were jobbers, small-scale wholesalers who bought goods from importers to sell to the trade. Only the very smallest establishments dealt with jobbers; larger ones could afford to import directly from Europe and the United States, while medium-sized shops dealt with wholesalers. Jews were more prominent in petty retail establishments—dry goods stores, men's furnishings, and tailor shops—than in wholesaling or manufacturing. Only in knit goods, where three of the twenty-two largest firms in metropolitan Buenos Aires were Jewish owned, did they appear at the industry's highest levels.[28]

As late as 1932, most clothes were still made in small shops from imported fabric.[29] There were, however, five spinning mills, with 45,000 spindles producing cotton yarn in Argentina. About 160 large and small mills were also using imported yarns to knit hosiery. Argentines wore very small quantities of cotton cloth (except duck), still less rayon, and almost no silk. Blankets and other cheap woolen goods were produced locally. Higher tariffs, instituted in two stages in 1930 and 1931, tended to restrict imports of cloth and expensive finished goods destined for sale in Buenos Aires' best shops and department stores. By the mid-1930s, hosiery, hats, and overcoats were being manufactured in fairly large factories but other clothes were still being produced in the workshops of retail department stores or the homes of small tailors and seamstresses.

Although in 1940 relatively primitive production processes continued to exist in Buenos Aires, the trend toward factory production was being stimulated by better protection of national industry and the availability of investment capital. As a result, the independent producer-merchant came under pressure either to shift up into manufacture or down into the factory. A few Jews had already successfully made the shift to manufacture, founding textile and clothing factories. By 1940, Jews owned thirty spinning and weaving mills and employed some 4,000 workers, many of whom were also Jewish. Jews also played an important role in the retail sale of woolen goods. In this field, in particular, Jewish entrepreneurs presided over the birth and expansion of a new industry, specializing in the production of sweaters, underwear, and bathrobes. Three large factories, sixty medium-sized establishments, and more than one hundred workshops shared production.[30] Most Jews, however, continued to make and sell products in the traditional fashion.

CARPENTRY

The Jews who disembarked in Buenos Aires at the end of the Nineteenth century needed inexpensive furniture as well as cheap clothing, and the first Jewish carpentry shops opened for business in 1894. Jews soon dominated the production of shoddy, gimcrack furniture in the city.[31] While the number of Jewish garment workers declined from 64 percent in the first sample of the Chevrah to 21 percent in the last, the percentage of furniture workers and carpenters rose consistently until it encompassed about a quarter of the working-class Jews in the 1930 sample.

As might be imagined, working conditions left much to be desired. Lathe operators labored twelve hours a day when there was work to be had. The majority of wood gilders worked nine hours each day, but the scarcity of work drove many out of the trade.

Furniture workers in first-class establishments tried to reduce their work day to eight hours and to eliminate piecework. In 1897, however, it was still impossible "to ascertain that the eight hour day had been established in all cases, owing in part to the negligence of personnel in the *boliches* [holes in the wall] where workers still did ten hours of work a day." The lowest level gimcrack furniture workshops were not shops at all. Instead they serviced auctioneers who offered the cheap furniture to the public. Such carpenters as these labored at piecework twelve to fourteen hours a day, earning three pesos for their efforts.[32]

Piecework in the trade began with the development of saw mills, which reduced construction costs and forced carpenters to work in their homes for less money. To make matters worse, all carpenters and furniture workers needed their own sets of tools, which cost about 200 pesos and represented a significant investment. But, according to Patroni "by this procedure human machinery has been able to compete with the mechanical.[33]

The shift of furniture makers to piecework and home production demonstrates that the sweatshop was by no means limited to the clothing industry. To take yet another example, in 1897 more than 6,000 Buenos Aires shoemakers worked in teams "each one doing a different job, mounting and finishing a pair of half-boots in a few minutes. These individuals work with the same celerity as a machine . . . scarcely making an average of three pesos a day."[34] Other trades were equally as susceptible to the perverse economics of the sweatshop. As the Argentine Department of Labor noted in 1915 (even though Argentine workers in several trades had experienced the evils of sweating for at least two decades):

> . . . we can assume that if it [the sweatshop] does not exist to any appreciable extent, the phenomenon will appear as the industries in our country progress. The embryo already exists. You can already see in . . . dressmaking establishments and salons . . . sufficient characteristics to consider these commerical houses, in many cases, as 'sweating enterprises.'

It defined the sweatshop as a workplace where "owners of establishments, generally small, work with the help of several seamstresses and apprentices. Unlike factories and workshops it is subject to a schedule which is neither systematic nor established because it is subject to the irregular demands placed on it by its clientele. These sites usually do not meet the health conditions recommended by hygiene."[35]

Exploitation of carpenters and other tradesmen in Argentina took other forms besides the sweatshop. Wage scales that provided equal pay for equal work were rare. Competition among workers for available jobs kept wages depressed. In small factories, manufacturers provided their foreman with ceiling costs for the production of each article. If the foreman was strict, practically everything could be made for less than the ceiling. The result was higher profits for the manufacturer, who generally allowed the foreman to keep a percentage of any savings. The factory system thus lent itself to speedups and other abuses.[36]

In spite of the hardships suffered by their workers, in 1904 immigrant Jewish concerns did an estimated four million pesos worth of business, the bulk of it split between clothing and furniture. Three years later, the total had risen dramatically, to seven million pesos. At the end of the decade, some 350 Jewish craftsmen made cheap tables, wardrobes, and upholstered furniture, employed some seven thousand workers, and controlled 70 percent of the gimcrack industry.[37]

Italian and Spanish craftworkers made what little high-quality furniture was produced domestically, but most finely worked furniture was imported. Argentine forests produced poor-quality lumber, and transportation costs from the interior to Buenos Aires ordinarily made production both inefficient and expensive. The fact that everything from hardware to glue had to be imported also kept prices high and volume low. However, the First World War made larger scale domestic production viable, at least temporarily, when imports declined. The war allowed Argentine workers to copy European styles and sell their work for high prices. But the boom passed quickly, and a recession in the construction industry threw 30,000 carpenters out of work. Many of the unemployed formed small companies and went into business for themselves or for retail stores. Self-employment, apparently, required only slightly more capital than did being a wage earner. The associated risks are suggested by the fact that for some self-employment was regarded not as upward mobility but as a last alternative to unemployment.[38]

The technological level of the trade was so low that almost all Argentine furniture was handmade. One observer noted that "very little machine work is done except roughing out the stock. The cabinet makers prepare the material and join it up and complete the piece for the finishers. Modern machines such as those for gluing and sanding, and other labor saving devices, are not used, and the hand labor done is considerable and costly."[39] Producers, for example, lacked both the equipment and the experience to make chairs, and before the war all but the very cheapest chairs were imported. The high costs of production meant that without protective tariffs Argentine furniture makers were unable to withstand the competition of imported machinemade chairs that undersold the domestic product after World War I. There was no tariff relief until 1930 and 1931, and by that time the Depression had intervened to create other difficulties.

Like other petty producers, Argentine furniture makers lacked capital. Many were "poor and unable to purchase modern machinery and stocks of supplies, or to manufacture in quantities to their own advantage."[40] As a result, the sweating system persisted in the furniture trades through at least the first three decades of the twentieth century.

Jewish carpenters and furniture makers produced for a market of limited funds. Because good furniture and bad furniture had separate markets, the two did not compete with each other. For several decades, the Jewish carpenter sold to a poor clientele and owed his success to the inexpensiveness of his product and to economies of labor.

As difficult as it was to progress in the garment industry, it was more difficult still for the carpenter. Only 14 percent of those Chevrah members who were carpenters who could be traced had become owners by 1927. Carpentry and furniture making required more investment than garment making, both in tools and space (and therefore in rents) and in physical labor, which reduced the extent to which families could contribute to the enterprise. In spite of frequent unemployment and of the obstacles to the entrepreneurial standing, however, there is no evidence that Jewish carpenters sought to abandon the trade.

JEWELRY

The jewelry trade, in contrast to carpentry and the needle trades, illustrates how different life was for the highly skilled and well paid who comprised only a small percentage of the Jewish working class. As in the case of the furniture industry, the relatively small domestic jewelry industry was stimulated when World War I cut off European sources of supply. *Porteño* jewelers produced fine pieces of platinum and 18-karat gold, while importers satisfied the demand for silver and gold plate. Generally, jewelers made gold, silver, and platinum chains as well as more decorative and expensive made-to-order pieces. They, too, copied European patterns rather than designing their own. Still, Argentines could not satisfy the demands of the market; in 1922, Argentina imported 5.5 million dollars worth of silverware and jewelry. By 1922, there were about forty jewelry shops in Buenos Aires with five or more employees. The largest employed about seventy craftsmen. Two Jewish firms ranked third and fourth in size and employed about twenty-five people each. The majority of the five or six hundred jewelry workers in Buenos Aires were immigrants who worked eight hours a day and received additional pay for overtime. Even though many domestic jewelers owed their success to their ability to undersell imports, they paid relatively high wages. Gold workers earned forty-five cents an hour and platinum workers half again as much. These businesses employed no salesmen, carried little or no stock, and kept overhead expenses to a minimum.[41]

Jewelry workers enjoyed conditions that existed nowhere else in the Jewish working class. Cigar and cigarette workshops, hidden as they often were behind tenements, were variations on the sweatshop theme. Leather workers suffered from the intense heat generated by tanning vats and from respiratory ailments caused by the lack of ventilation. All other workers dreaded tuberculosis and other occupationally related diseases, as well as industrial accidents.

Jewelers were better able to consolidate their nonmanual positions than their counterparts in the garment and furniture industries, a fact suggesting that to a significant degree entrepreneurial success was a function of a worker's level of skill. Though some occupational inconsistency existed even among jewelers, in general, the more skilled the trade, the less critical the factors that contributed to the collapse of small businesses.

STREET VENDING

The Argentine tradition of paying cash for goods necessarily left the *porteño* poor on the fringes of the market. The conjuncture of waves of eastern European Jewish immigration and the low level of Argentine industrialization and merchandising offered Jews the opportunity to cater to these previously neglected consumers. In street peddling and petty commerce, which were based in large part on the existence of credit, Jews already familiar with such techniques in Europe had a distinct advantage in Argentina.

In Argentina, street vendors were called "cuentaniks" (a combination of the Spanish word cuenta, or account, and the Yiddish suffix) or "klappers" (door knockers). Most sold on credit. Carrying their goods on horseback or on a wagon or on their shoulders, they covered the city's tenements, its suburbs, and the Argentine interior ready to sell to anyone who paid whatever he could. Preceded by their traditional call "spreads and quilts" often in broken Spanish, they sold a wide variety of other products.[42]

In a remarkable memoir published in the left-wing Peronist magazine *Las Bases,* a non-Jewish Argentine recalled the Jewish peddler of the 1930s as "wonderful; beloved and respected and [who] today . . . is something truly inconceivable." One particular peddler, known only by his sobriquet "the Russian," walked through tenements with his samples and left with stacks of bills for his customers to pay "whenever you can." He was a man of "good faith, who required no signatures, who didn't know what a guarantee meant, who trusted in people." The tenement dwellers of the 1930s were unable collectively to raise 100 pesos, but "the Russian" went to them nonetheless. "That was his business and they were his clients. Such men were the economic bulwarks of the working class. They brought to the tenements a boy's first suit of clothes, a kitchen table and chairs, and a ring for a girl's fifteenth birthday—all for one peso a week without guarantees."[43]

This reminiscence is no doubt romanticized. As credit selling became more widely accepted, and as goods previously available from street vendors became readily accessible elsewhere, the street vendor became obsolete. By the mid-1920s, if not earlier, house-to-house peddling had become a form of begging rather than a commerce.

Street vendors faced major problems. As retail establishments in Buenos Aires prospered, department stores hired traveling salesmen of their own to saturate the interior. They also began mail-order businesses that competed with the vendors. The city of Buenos Aires regulated street vendors in 1901, 1911, and 1917 and in the spirit of reform greatly circumscribed their activities.[44] Most serious, street vendors had to contend with a significant percentage of delinquent clients and wholesalers who charged them high prices.

To protect themselves from wholesalers, the cuentaniks formed protective associations. Although many of the early ones failed, their history provides some insights into the problems they attempted to address. Membership in the League for the Defense of Argentine Jewish Commerce, for example, was limited to those "who sell merchandise on their own, in weekly or monthly installments, without having an established store." In October 1915, seven cuentaniks established the Jewish Vendors Union, open only to those who spoke Yiddish. After the war, the association added a cooperative to provide goods at lower and more stable prices than were available from wholesalers. In 1916, several street vendors founded the Jewish League of Commercial Defense and Mutual Aid to "provide its members with first quality goods at fair prices." Among the League's other aims were protecting members' economic interests and organizing conferences to educate and solicit other vendors. The League also protected its members against exploitation by wholesalers, helped them to obtain credit, and assisted their families in time of illness or death. Finally, it established an information office to let members know, among other things, about customers behind in their payments.[45] In 1919, the association issued shares of 100 pesos, payable in ten installments. The League's instability is revealed by the fact that even the biggest peddlers bought only five shares each. Nevertheless, a decade later, the League had purchased a building costing $400,000. Many other cooperatives were established in the next several years.[46]

Slowly, with the aid of cooperatives and associations, some street vendors opened stores or founded businesses. In the 1930s, Simon Weill, director of the Jewish Colonization Association in Argentina, found that "the number of traders includes those who until only a short while ago were simple peddlers who sold on credit and were known as 'cuentaniks.' [Some] established their own retail or wholesale stores and now sell on credit much less than formerly."[47] The others continued to struggle. The lament of Emilio Serta's fictional cuentanik in the 1930s illustrated their plight: "in all three pesos of sales and one of profit, [and] to obtain this pittance it is necessary to suffer the heat. . . ."[48] Whatever improvements in "working conditions" they enjoyed were due to their own efforts rather than to legislation.

The numerical importance of street vendors increased as their commercial role declined. Street vendors constituted only two percent of the nonmanuals in the 1905–1910 sample. Only three sample members identified themselves as street vendors when they joined the Chevrah in 1914–1915. By contrast, street vendors represented fully 37 percent of the nonmanuals in the 1930 sample.

Street vendors had a difficult time accumulating capital, most likely because they lacked skills and sufficient knowledge of the market to enter business successfully. No more than one-fifth of those who joined the Chevrah as cuentaniks ever owned their own stores, though many others eventually entered and remained in the working class.

Occupational patterns of Jews in Buenos Aires were generally characterized by seasonal unemployment, declining rates of upward mobility, occupational inconsistency, and underemployment. In no case were these factors more important than in that of the cuentaniks. Their inability to save and their increasing resort to manual occupations in an era of growing commercial sophistication more than suggest the marginality of the street vendors.

SMALL BUSINESS

Most of the Jewish community was composed of workers and small shopkeepers who shared similar problems. As a practical matter, mobility was usually limited to crossing the line between worker and owner (often more than once).

Analyses of small business mortality at five- or ten-year intervals between 1895 and 1947, based on the Chevrah's records, city directories, commercial guides and almanacs, and telephone books, reveal the fragile basis underlying the movement of skilled workers to nonmanual positions. In this respect, Argentina was not unlike other countries; data from the United States, organized by city and by trade, indicate that the majority of small U.S. businesses that opened between 1843 and 1936 lasted only three years. Retail establishments had longer lifetimes than craft or service businesses but shorter lifetimes than wholesalers or manufacturing concerns. There is also, in the U.S. data, a positive relationship between business survival and a stagnant population; thus the greater the population growth and the larger the city, the higher the number of failures.[49]

In Buenos Aires, with its ever increasing population, a high rate of business mortality could be forecast at all times. In 1910 and 1914, for instance, business failures in Argentina averaged almost 67 million dollars, or about 7.40 dollars per person. In the United States, failures averaged only 2.55 dollars per person during the same time period.[50]

On a continuum, individually owned businesses fail more frequently and more rapidly than partnerships, whereas corporations outlive jointly owned businesses. The preponderance of singly owned Jewish business testifies to the small-scale nature of Jewish commerce in Buenos Aires. For instance, the majority of those enumerated in the 1895 census who owned businesses in 1917 did so alone. Few Jews ever formed partnerships and fewer still participated in corporations. It is logical to assume, considering cross-cultural similarities, that the natural and market forces that influenced business mortality in other countries also affected enterprises in Buenos Aires and that individually owned businesses had the highest mortality rate in Argentina.

Only one of the nine Jewish partnerships existing in 1921 included a nonfamily member, indicating the importance of the extended family in entrepreneurship and capital accumulation. Still further evidence of the petty bougeois nature of the community is that only two of thirty-one businesses operated at two locations in that year. By 1927, one more businessman had opened a second store, while another owned two different businesses at the same address. Seven Jews participated in multiple ownerships, two of them in corporations.[51]

A sample-by-sample analysis of Jewish businesses demonstrates the constant ebb and flow of Jewish fortunes in Buenos Aires. Slightly more than 10 percent of those who joined the Chevrah between 1905 and 1910 owned their own businesses in 1917. Rafael N., a glove maker, was typical of the majority in that he was a sole owner. Gregorio R. owned a pawnshop in 1917; a decade later, at the same address, he gave his occupation as a tailor, reflecting the phenomenon of sole ownership, as well as the decline of a Jewish presence in the pawnshop business and relatively easy entry into the garment industry. Jacobo A., owner of a furniture making factory, was the only member of the sample in business with a nonrelative, although his partnership proved temporary; by 1923, he was in business alone.

In 1927, the last year of the Alvear administration—a period of some prosperity—fully 51 percent of the second sample were in business. The vast majority were sole owners, with only 21 percent of these businessmen participating in some form of multiple ownership. By 1927, only 4.7 percent of these entrepreneurs owned more than one business site. Isaac S. was one of an even smaller minority with three sites. Isaac and his brother owned one parquet factory at Lavalle 3593, a second at Guardia Vieja 3532, and an office at Callao 714, from which they imported wood and presumably managed their affairs. As partners, the brothers were unusual in that even at the height of Jewish entrepreneurial activity in 1927, 85 percent were sole owners.

Those who joined the Chevrah in 1914 and 1915, the third sample, reflected similar traits. In 1917, Lazaro L., a commissions agent, was one of only thirteen sample members in business. By 1920, he was making brass beds and several years later he owned a factory that made mattresses. This last effort was apparently more successful than previous ones because he was still at it in 1936. Four years later, only three of the twenty-two Jews in business were part owners. For this group, too, 1927 was the high point of commercial expansion, with 36 percent of the sample in the nonmanual ranks. Jacobo W., a carpenter who joined the Chevrah when he was thirty, was one of eight sample members who participated in partnerships and was one of four in business with a nonrelative. He and his partner owned a carpentry shop at L. Viale 336, where Jacobo was living when he died in 1936. In 1927, ninety-eight of those in business operated at one location, only three operated at two. These same patterns held true a decade later—single locations and sole ownerships predominated.

Of the three percent of those in the 1920 sample who had businesses in 1921, five were sole owners and three shared control of their concerns with relatives. By 1927, about one quarter of the sample had entered business, the majority of them sole owners like Israel Y. He joined the Chevrah at age thirty-four, giving his occupation as a carpenter. After seven years he had prospered to the point where he owned a furniture shop in Bartolome Mitre 3218. When Gabriel C. joined the Chevrah he was single and twenty-four. He too was a carpenter, but he had a distinct advantage over others—by 1927 his father had taken him as a business partner. The firm had a factory at Cangallo 4445–4447 and a showroom at Bernardo de Irigoyen 573—one of seven businesses, or 10 percent of the sample, that operated two locations. Eighty percent of the enterprises were individually owned. A similarly high percentage obtained in 1936.

Fewer than one fifth of those who joined the Chevrah in 1925 had established businesses which they advertised in the 1927 directory of the Jewish community. Some 94 percent of the sample members listed as businessmen were sole owners. Three people participated in multiple ownerships; two of whom shared control with a nonrelative. Mauricio J. was typical in most respects of Jewish businessmen in this sample. Forty years old, married, and the father of two teenaged children when he joined the Chevrah, Mauricio had lived in Buenos Aires for two decades, although he differed from others in that he had emigrated from Russia to neighboring Chile before crossing the Andes into Argentina. In business alone, he maintained a fur shop less than a block from his home at Bartolomé Mitre 2345. Jacob S was the one sample member who owned two business locations. His rise was all the more unusual for the fact that he came to Argentina in 1923. Only four years after his emigration from Russia, Jacob owned a clothing store at Corrientes 2473 and a tailor shop at Córdoba 648, which supported his wife and infant daughter. But a year later, he was in business only at the Corrientes location. The 1936 trace revealed that none of the twenty-two entrepreneurs who joined the Chevrah in 1925 had two or more sites. Two had formed partnerships with nonrelatives and one owned shares in a simple corporation.

The 1936 Buenos Aires telephone directory listed some sixty-one members of the 1930 sample. None had two business locations, only six were involved in partnerships, and one in a corporation. Even in 1945, none of the sixty-six found from the 1930 sample had been able to open a second location. Single ownership remained the dominant form of commerce.

As suggested in data from all the samples, businesses that require the least capital investment have the highest mortality rates because the small entrepreneur cannot afford to study the market or hire experienced help. The entire undertaking commonly suffers from a lack of business experience. The small businessman, historically, enters overcrowded fields and faces stiff competition.

While in some cases the little capital that was obtained contributed to a longer business life, persistence should not be confused with prosperity. Even though the petty entrepreneur purchased on short-term credit, reduced rental costs by using his residence as his workplace, and kept labor costs to a minimum by hiring women and children or relying on the labor of his family, profits still remained small. In such cases, businesses may not have actually failed, but earnings were so low that families were just barely able to survive.

The absence of surplus capital was an important cause of Argentine business mortality. In 1919, the U. S. Department of Commerce reported that

> one of the handicaps in the normal development of any country's industries and resources is the lack of capital in sufficient quantities. This is particularly true in Argentina. Many undertakings based on sound business projects have failed for lack of funds to keep them going until they

are established. Factory industries cannot be initiated without the necessary financial support to permit economy of production, since it is on that basis that they must compete with the imported articles. Up to the present the tremendous growth of agricultural and stockraising industries yielding relatively prompt and large profits has absorbed nearly all the surplus capital in Argentina.[52]

The difficulties of capital accumulation caused significant problems for aspiring entrepreneurs. In a frequently repeated opinion, the U.S. Department of Commerce reported that "to operate on any but a very small scale requires a disproportionately large amount of capital. Thousands of pesos will be tied up in payments, freights, and especially in customs duties. Orders for material have to be placed months in advance, and it requires judgment and foresight to avoid losses through changed market conditions, modifications in design, etc. Disappointing delays occur in the arrival of goods and at times these cause serious losses."[53]

One way to accumulate at least some capital was to work intensely hard where and when there was money to be made. With this in mind, a number of *porteño* Jews turned their eyes on the interior. Demand for rural labor was almost always high, and the government continually sought to channel immigrants to the interior. It is likely that enterprising urban residents took advantage of the harvest's high wages and low cost of living to accumulate capital. The *golondrinas,* the seasonal laborers who crossed the ocean to work in the harvest, earned the cost of their passage from Europe in two weeks in the fields. Whatever else they earned during their three- or four-month sojourns on the pampas, less minimal expenses, represented profits. Wages earned during the harvest helped to finance the medical education of young Russian Jewish immigrant Enrique Dickmann and, doubtless, contributed to the establishment of several small businesses.[54] By 1925, however, mechanization of the agricultural sector had reached a sufficiently high level to discourage seasonal migration, closing one avenue of capital accumulation.

The nature of the Argentine banking system reinforced the difficulty of obtaining capital. By 1910, the Banco de la Nación directly controlled about one-third of all banking and had indirect control over another third. Poor harvests in 1910 and 1911 served to further strengthen the power of the Banco de la Nación at the expense of other banks. The national bank loaned only to those who had the best credit ratings and could provide significant collateral. This served to eliminate all but the most solvent from access to the bank's capital. Thus, according to Joseph Tulchin, "the Argentine credit system tended to focus financial power on the Banco de la Nación and favor those directly connected with the exports of cereals and meats. Any effort to alter the credit system would threaten the economic groups which benefitted from it, and prompt them to sally forth to defend their interests."[55]

If government institutions preferred to lend to large cattle ranchers, foreign banks were quite willing to support their national interests. Neither was favorably inclined toward poor businessmen or aspiring entrepreneurs. Cooperatives, voluntary associations, and immigrant banks sought to fill the void. In 1917, a group of Jewish immigrants, starting with 120 pesos, founded the Industrial Bank (thought to be the first Argentine bank to provide loans to potential manufacturers). In 1930, the Depression notwithstanding, the Industrial Bank made loans of 270,000 dollars, while a second bank founded through the efforts of ten workers and entrepreneurs loaned nearly 2 million dollars. Between 1917 and 1931, another eight Jewish banks were established, and by 1945, twenty-nine banks, cooperatives, and commercial associations provided credit within the community. These organizations "began as credit institutions typically of the ghetto until they took on the form of true banks."[56] The Jewish character of the banks was reflected in such names as the Banco Israelita de Rí de la Plata, in the composition of their boards of directors, and in their contributions to the community's charities.

THOSE WHO PROSPERED

Until industralization, stimulated by import-substitution policies, finally generated the beginnings of opportunity, and until a need arose for trained personnel, commerce and petty trade offered Jews the most likely avenues for advancement. In his study *Those Who Rule*, sociologist José Luis de Imaz argued that Jews "internalized the norms for 'ascetic bourgeoisies'" and became innovators and modernizers.[57] The latter contention seems more justifiable than the former. Jews introduced and participated in changes in productive processes, created new spheres of activity in older industries, and pioneered in credit selling. Some accumulated fortunes in the process.

Most Jews were much less fortunate. The vast majority of Jews in Buenos Aires were so poor that their estates never attracted the attention of the authorities and were never probated. To the best of our knowledge only seven of the sixty-six sample members known to have died in Buenos Aires between 1896 and 1932 left wills. Six of the seven were living in Buenos Aires in 1895 and one arrived in 1913.[58]

Six of the seven were tradesmen when they died. Four of them owned their own homes while two also owned other urban property. One owned his workshop but rented his residence.

One of the seven *comerciantes* listed himself as a peon in 1895. In 1917, he called himself an auctioneer. When he died he left his heir an unappraised house at Bernardo de Irigoyen 1241 (also his business address) and 5,000 pesos. He also left furniture worth 485 pesos. A second tradesman owned five urban properties worth 216,000 pesos, mortgaged for 39,000 pesos. When he died in 1923, he had only 16.77 pesos in the bank. The community recognized his eminence and in 1900 and 1906 elected him to office in the Chevrah. The third *comerciante* fell somewhere in between. He owned his own home, worth 20,000 pesos, and left movable property worth 350 pesos and the same amount in cash.

In 1895, the fourth tradesman, was thirty-seven, single, propertyless, and employed as a shoe closer. When he died twelve years later he manufactured shoes. He rented his home but owned a lot in Puente Alsina, a city in Buenos Aires province, worth almost 3,000 pesos. In addition, he held 3,000 pesos in stocks, had 255 pesos in the bank, and was owed 1,000 pesos.

José Luis R. remained a tinsmith until his death in 1923. In 1895 he owned no property. Almost three decades later he left one unappraised property—his workshop—around the corner from his home, some old clothes, and ten watches.

The last tradesman, a tailor, was the most successful of all those whose wills were probated. He owned three properties, including his home, in Buenos Aires. He owned three additional lots in Buenos Aires province. The urban property was worth almost 220,000 pesos (mortgaged for 75,000); the rural land was valued at 8,800 pesos. He was 30,000 pesos in debt but owned 35,000 pesos worth of a tailor shop "La sin rival." This entrepreneurial success was also recognized when he was elected to office in the Chevrah in 1906.

That these Jews are atypical is clear. Published census data indicate that very few Jews owned property. In fact, in spite of their early eminence in trade and industry, immigrants in general owned less than half the available real estate in 1885. By 1914, immigrants owned about 60 percent of the real estate in the city. Jews, however, owned only one percent of the total.[59]

On the basis of the seven probates we know about, it appears that those Jews with money, rather than building up reserves of cash or jewelry, invested in urban property, almost all of it in outlying neighborhoods. Thus, successful Jews were not aloof from the urban land speculation rife in Buenos Aires in the first three decades of the present century. This preference for land and their small cash reserves offer some insight into the liquidity crisis in Argentine finance. Inflation, then as now, made saving unprofitable, and all available cash was invested in land. Land also probably served as collateral for the purchase of additional real estate, stock, and inventories.

The activities of prosperous Jews in Argentina bear little resemblance to the stereotype of small businessmen hoarding liquid, easily hidden, and easily carried assets. In their investments and speculations, those few Jews who did accumulate assets usually succumbed to the lure of the land, exactly as other *porteños* of means did.

Notes

1. For a complete discussion of the occupational classification system used: *see:* Mark D. Szuchman and Eugene F. Sofer, "The State of Occupational Stratification Studies in Argentina: A Classificatory Scheme," *Latin American Research Review,* XI (Spring, 1976), 159–172.

1a. E. P. Thompson, *The Making of the English Working Class* (New York: Vintage, 1966), p. 248.

2. George E. Barnett, *Chapters on Machinery and Labor* (Carbondale: Southern Illinois University Press, 1969), p. 117.

3. Wilbert E. Moore, "Technological Change and the Worker," Simon Marcson, ed., *Automation, Alienation, and Anomie* (New York: Harper & Row, 1970), p. 50.

4. On entrepreneurship, *see:* Hugh G. J. Aitken, ed., *Explorations in Enterprise* (Cambridge: Harvard University Press, 1967), Bert F. Hoselitz, *Sociological Aspects of Economic Growth* (New York: The Free Press, 1960), Seymour Martin Lipset, "Values, Education and Entrepreneurship," Seymour Martin Lipset and Aldo Solari, eds., *Elites in Latin America* (New York: Oxford University Press, 1956), pp. 3–60, which has an excellent bibliography and Ivan H. Light, *Ethnic Enterprise in America* (Berkeley: University of California Press, 1972).

5. Elias Tcherikower, ed. *The Early Jewish Labor Movement in the United States* (New York: YIVO, 1961), p. 11.

6. The United States Census of 1900, for example, reported that more than half of the masons and plasters and nearly as many brick and tile workers were unemployed part of the year. Forty percent of all carpenters and 27 percent of all tailors were without work part of 1900. *See:* Isaac A. Hourwich, *Immigration and Labor* (New York: B. W. Huebsch, Inc., 1922), pp. 114–115.

7. United States, Department of Commerce, *The Economic Position of Argentina During the War* (Washington: Government Printing Office, 1920), p. 11. The 1914 Argentine census neglected to ask respondents whether they were unemployed. Its designer felt that "this would have photographed a social status which was not the

normal one and would have led, in an immigration country, to erroneous conclusions." Nevertheless, an incisive observer nevertheless estimated that there were some 410,000 people, most of them in Buenos Aires and its environs, who were unemployed in 1914. Most of the idle were artisans and persons "collaborating with industry." Felix Weil, *The Argentine Riddle* (New York: John Day Co., 1944), 327. Also see: Adrián Patroni, *Los trabajadores en la Argentina* (Buenos Aires: n.p., 1897) pp. 22, 24, 30, 84, and 85, Pablo Storni "La industria y la situación de las clases obreras en la Capital de la República," *Revista Juridica de ciencias sociales*, 25 (October-December 1908), 260, and Great Britain, Department of Overseas Trade, *Economic Conditions in the Argentine Republic,* November 1929 (London: H. M. Stationery Office, 1929), p. 7.

8. Samuel Halphon in Jewish Colonization Association, *Rapport,* (1909), pp. 305–307.

9. República Argentina, Departmento Nacional del Trabajo., *Boletín,* 30 (April 1915), p. 76.

10. República Argentina, Departmento Nacional del Trabajo. *Boletín* 29 (Diciembre 1914), 82.

11. On the development of the clothing industry, *see:* Louis Levine, *The Women's Garment Workers* (New York: B. W. Huebsch Inc., 1924), Charles E. Zaretz, *The Amalgamated Clothing Workers of America* (New York: Ancon Publishers, 1934), and Joel Seidman, *The Needle Trades* (New York: Farrar and Rinehart, 1942).

12. United States, Department of Commerce. *Wearing Apparel in Argentina* (Washington D.C.: Government Printing Office, 1918), pp. 47–48.

13. John R. Commons, "The Sweating System in the Clothing Trade," 319–320, ed. John R. Commons, *Trade Unions and Labor Problems* (Boston: Ginn and Co., 1905), p. 327.

14. República Argentina, Departmento Nacional del Trabajo, *Boletín,* 3 (Diciembre 1907), p. 328.

15. United States, Department of Commerce, *Textile Markets of Argentina, Uruguay, and Paraguay* (Washington D.C.: Government Printing Office, 1920) p. 17.

16. M. Benario, "El comercio y la industria judío en Buenos Aires," in *Homenaje a "El Diario Israelita"* (Buenos Aires: Comite de Homenaje a *"El Diario Israelita,"* 1940), p. 75.

17. República Argentina, Departmento Nacional del Trabajo, *Boletín,* 3 (Diciembre 1907), p. 328.

18. See José Panettieri, *Los trabajadores* (Buenos Aires: Jorge Alvarez, 1968), p. 80. On the evils of sweating in New York, *see:* Jacob Riis, *How the Other Half Lives* (New York: Hill and Wang, 1957). For London, *see:* Beatrice Webb, "The Diary of an Investigator," and "The Jews of East London," in Sidney and Beatrice Webb, *Problems of Modern Industry* (London: Longman, Green, and Co., 1898), pp. 1–19 and 20–45.

19. Beatrice Potter (Webb) in Charles Booth, *Life and Labour of the People in London,* vol. 4 (London: Macmillan and Co., 1892), p. 40.

20. Félix de Ugarteche, *Las industrias del cuero en la República Argentina* (Buenos Aires: Talleres Graficas de Roberto Canals, 1927), p. 397.

21. Sweating is defined as "unusually low rates of wages, excessive hours of labour, and insanitary workplaces," in Webb, *Problems of Modern Industry,* p. 140. One expert on the clothing industry argues that the sweatshop will always be a characteristic of the industry. *See:* Zaretz, *The Amalgamated Clothing Workers,* p. 32.

22. Quoted in Panettieri, *Los trabajadores,* p. 80.

23. Ibid., p. 80.

24. Commons, "The Sweating System," pp. 319–320.

25. J.A. Garrad, *The English and Immigration, 1880–1910* (London: Oxford University Press, 1971), p. 173; H. Brusilovsky, "Los Judíos en el movimiento obrero Argentino," in *Homenaje a "El Diario Israelita,"* p. 97, and Tcherikower, *The Early Jewish Labor Movement.*

26. Sample data. In London, for example, Charles Booth noted that "the case with which a man may become a master is proverbial . . . . His living room becomes his workshop, his landlord or his butcher his security; round the corner he finds a brother Israelite whose trade is to supply pattern garments to take as samples of work to the wholesale house; with a small deposit he secures on the hire system both sewing machine and presser's table. Altogether it is estimated that with one pound sterling in his pocket any many rise to the dignity of a sweater." In *Life and Labour,* vol. 4, p. 60. Booth also reported that: "to begin quite alone, either in the home, or by hiring a bench in a workshop, is . . . a frequent practice, and it is one of the drawbacks of that trade that men can so easily do this, and after having helped to 'degrade' the market for a time, fall back again into the ranks of wage-earners . . . . For others, this step is the starting point of a permanent change in position, that may or may not turn out to be improvement. It would be misleading, however, to leave the impression that all who start on their own account do so quite voluntarily ; . . . A large class therefore 'start for themselves' because they cannot get employment and to start thus, even though sale by hawking or sale by auction is a man's only resource, becomes in these circumstances a natural and even a necessary thing to do. . . . Many small makers . . . begin on a capital of one pound sterling." In *Life and Labour,* vol. 4, pp. 176–177.

27. United States, Department of Commerce, *Wearing Apparel,* p. 23.

28. United States, Department of Commerce, *Wearing Apparel,* pp. 123–128.

Type of Clothing	Firms	Firms in B.A. (#)	Jewish Firms (#)	Jewish in B.A. (#)
Shirts, collars, cuffs	12	12	—	—
Exterior clothing	17	9	—	—
White goods	7	4	—	—
Knit goods	22	20	3	1
Corsets	4	4	—	—

Also *see:* United States, Department of Commerce, *Textile Market of Argentina* (Washington, D.C.: Government Printing Office, 1932), p. 103. Another indication of the still small-scale nature of the industry is the distribution of sewing machines in the city of Buenos Aires. Local sewing machine merchants estimated "that there are only six or eight clothing firms in Buenos Aires which operate over 100 sewing machines in their own factories, the largest one being about 300 machines on Government uniform orders, followed by the Government's own uniform factory with about 250 machines." United States, Department of Commerce, *Textile Market of Argentina,* p. 38.

29. United States, *Textile Market of Argentina,* p. 7.

30. Bernario, "El comercio y la industria," p. 76.

31. Benario, "El comercio y la industria," p. 75 and *Enciclopedia Judaica Castellana* (Mexico: Editorial Enciclopedia Judaica Castellana, 1948) vol. I, p. 442.

32. Patroni, *Los trabajadores,* p. 85.

33. The first Jewish saw mill was opened in 1907. By 1940, Jews owned approximately one-third of the total in Buenos Aires. *Enciclopedia Judaica Castellana,* vol. I, p. 443. Also *see:* Patroni, *Los trabajadores,* p. 85.

34. Patroni, *Los trabajadores,* pp. 92–93.

35. República Argentina, Departmento Nacional del Trabajo. *Boletín* 30 (April 1915), p. 80.

36. United States, Department of Commerce, *Wearing Apparel,* p. 129.

37. Bernario, "El comercio y la industria," p. 75 and *Enciclopedia Judaica Castellana,* vol. I, p. 442.

38. United States, Department of Commerce, *Furniture Markets of Argentina, Uruguay, Paraguay, and Brazil* (Washington, D.C.: Government Printing Office, 1919), p. 24.

39. United States, Department of Commerce, *Furniture Markets of Argentina,* p. 24.

40. United States, Department of Commerce, *Furniture Markets of Argentina,* p. 25.

41. United States, Department of Commerce, *Jewelry and Silverware in Argentina, Uruguay, and Brazil* (Washington D.C.: Government Printing Office, 1922), pp. 6–7.

42. On street vendors in Argentina, *see:* Sociedad Comercial e Industrial Israelita, *45 aniversario* (Buenos Aires: Sociedad Comercial e Industrial Argentina, 1961), M. Barres, *Male sociales* (Buenos Aires: Imprenta Lopez, 1939), pp. 60–61, and Pinie Wald, *The Jewish Working Class and Socialist Movements in Argentina* (Buenos Aires: Asociación Mutual Israelita, 1963), pp. 6–7. In Yiddish.

43. *Las Bases,* July 16, 1974, pp. 2–3.

44. In 1901, and again in 1917, the city regulated the conduct and dress of food vendors. It also provided that no vendor could have a contagious disease and limited the activity of vendors in the center city to the period between dawn and noon. Buenos Aires, *Digesto Municipal, 1936* (Buenos Aires: Municipalidad de Buenos Aires, 1936), p. 1049. In 1911, the city restricted activity in the area between 25 de Mayo, Balcarce, Belgrano, Bernardo de Irigoyen, Carlos Pellegrini, and Lavalle to the hours between noon and six p.m. It further required all street vendors except book, magazine, and newspaper salesmen to get a certificate of good health from the city. *Digesto Municipal, 1936,* p. 860.

45. Sociedad Comercial e Industrial Israelita, *45 aniversario,* pp 1–3.

46. The sociedad Comercial e Industrial apparently contributed to an improvement in its members' economic status. Yet, the 1930 Depression forced the association "to reduce its activities, given that a large percentage of members retired, unable to fulfill their obligations, in spite of the fact that the directors aided them with special credits and facilities, *45 aniversario* p. 3.

47. Simon Weill, *La Población israelita en la Republica Argentina* (Buenos Aires: Bene Berith, 1936), p. 15.

48. Emilio Serta, *Judíos de Buenos Aires* (Buenos Aires: Ediciones Feria, n.d.) p. 75.

49. *See:* R.G. and A.R. Hutchinson and Mabel Newcomer, "A Study in Business Mortality," *American Economic Review* XXVIII (September 1938), 511.

50. Roger W. Babson, *The Future of South America* (Boston: Little, Brown & Co., 1916), p. 205.

51. These data are the result of tracing the 1,500 randomly sampled members of the Chevrah through a variety of sources to determine their ownership patterns where possible. In the absence of data regarding incomes, other variables act as surrogates. The form of business—single ownership, partnership with a relative or nonfamily member, or corporation—suggests the level of sophistication involved. The number of business locations is intended to serve as at least a rough index of entrepreneurial success and prosperity.

52. United States, Department of Commerce, *Boots and Shoes* (1919), p. 45.

53. Ibid., p. 45.

54. Enrique Dickmann, *Recuerdos de un militante socialista* (Buenos Aires: La Vanguardia 1949), p. 44.

55. Joseph Tulchin, "Agricultural Credit and Politics in Argentina, 1910–1922," (unpublished paper, n.d.), pp. 6–7.

56. Jacob Shatzky, *Communidades judias en latinoamérica* (Buenos Aires: Ediciones del American Jewish Committee, 1952), p. 44.

57. José Luis de Imaz, *Los Que Mandan,* translated by Carlos A. Astiz (Albany: State University of New York Press, 1970), p. 151.

58. Probates located in Archivo de Tribunales, Buenos Aires.

59. República Argentina, Comision nacional del censo. *Tercer censo nacional (1914),* vol. 4, (Buenos Aires: Talleres Graficos de L. J. Rosso y Cia, 1916), p. 6.

CHAPTER 6   CONCLUSION

The election of Juan Domingo Perón in 1946, due in large part to his working-class and nationalist rhetoric, ushered in a new era for Argentina. It was under Perón that the first truly significant changes in Argentina's social structure took place. His populist conception of an industrialized Argentina organized into a multiclass alliance in which continued prosperity would ameliorate inevitable class tensions did much to change the traditional Argentine system.

Peronism had an enormous and largely beneficial impact on the Jewish community. But in 1945 Perón seemed to be just another military man of unbridled ambition, nationalist fervor, and anti-Semitic tendencies. During his presidential campaign, some of Perón's supporters roamed through Jewish neighborhoods, beating people and desecrating synagogues and community institutions. Contemporaries reported Jewish fears of a full-fledged pogrom. Protests were answered by official condemnations of anti-Semitism, but the attacks continued. In a highly charged atmosphere, exacerbated by demogoguery and the intervention on behalf of Perón's rivals of U.S. ambassador Spruille Braden, Perón was elected president.

Between his election and inauguration, Perón abandoned the policies of the junta. Although attempts to reassure the Jewish community were made and some liberties, such as the use of Yiddish in public meetings, were restored, anti-Jewish propaganda and the fear it provoked continued. Jews were also upset by the declaration that Argentina would permit selected workers, "especially agricultural workers and technicians" from "Italy, Spain, Ireland and the Low Countries," to immigrate at a time when thousands of Jews displaced by World War II were desperately seeking homes.[1] Between 1946 and the first quarter of 1947, only 450 Jewish immigrants entered the country. At the end of 1948, however, the Argentine Congress granted an amnesty to all foreigners who had entered the country without visas, and the next year several thousand Jews, among other recent arrivals, took advantage of the opportunity to settle legally in Argentina.

As a result of its wartime neutrality, Argentina had amassed unprecedentedly large gold reserves that it soon spent. Its import substitution policies developed and further improved the position of the nascent national bourgeoisie. The working class, the chief beneficiaries of Peronist populism, received a larger share of an expanded pie. The light industries, especially textiles and wearing apparel in which Jews figured prominently, benefited from the protection of the state. These policies heightened the importance of the Confederación General Económico (CGE), founded in 1951 under Peronist auspices to represent the interests of the national bourgeoisie. In *Those Who Rule,* José Luis de Imaz located six Jews of eastern European origin in the front ranks of the CGE in 1953 and 1963, a much higher percentage than that found in the leadership ranks of organizations with strong ties to foreign capital.[2] None of these prominent Jewish entrepreneurs had any higher education.

Despite uninterrupted anti-Semitic agitation by right-wing nationalists, in 1949 the American Jewish Committee reported that "by and large, . . . the Jewish community had little cause for complaint."[3] Perón's pro-Jewish stand, suspect in 1945, had become an integral part of his policies. After 1948, he maintained tolerably cordial relations with the Jewish community and managed to be both pro-Israel and friendly to the Arab nations. Perón's wife, Eva, stated her husband's official position that "in our country the only ones who have separated us by religion have been the representatives of the . . . oligarchy. Those who caused anti-Semitism were the rulers who poisoned the people with false theories."[4]

Jews could be pleased about the legislative prohibition on racial agitation, about Argentina's significant beef exports to Israel while those to Europe were curtailed, and about improved relations between government agencies and independent Jewish organizations. Nevertheless, Jews, so far as can be determined, refrained from voting for Peronist candidates. In the November 1951 congressional elections for example, Jewish Peronists were defeated by Jewish Radicals in what were considered largely Jewish districts.

Because anti-Semites did not find themselves in the mainstream of Argentine politics during the Perón regime, Perón's overthrow in 1955 led to an upsurge rather than a diminution of anti-Semitism. The attitudes of the nationalist right toward Perón and his movement are instructive in this regard. Some nationalists almost immediately became disaffected from Perón and opposed his candidacy. Marcelo Sanchez Sorondo recalled that "for me, Perón was not the Leader. He went in for working class demogogy . . . which could have exacerbated the class struggle and led to a civil war." The progressive dissatisfaction of anti-Semitic priest Julio Meinville reveals the Catholic right's growing hostility to Perón. Meinville opposed Perón's selective nationalism because it was "not integrated into a universal conception of Christian values," and he believed that Perón's indifference to Christianity was leading him toward Marxism. In 1950, the priest accused the regime of "totalitarianism and collectivism."[5]

Perón's fall from power was in large part due to a split in approaches to Argentine economic development that has characterized the country for most of this century. Broadly speaking, two antithetical modes of development, each with powerful supporters, have marked modern Argentine history. The first, the preserve of Argentine liberals and oligarchs, understands the country to be essentially agricultural. Wealth, and the political power that accompanies it, should be concentrated, they contend, in the hands of an elite. Perón most fully articulated the second mode between 1946 and 1955, when he sought to make Argentina a more democratic society in terms of social class and income redistribution, although he was strongly influenced by corporatist and antiliberal ideologies. Under this conception, the state becomes the guarantor of social welfare and the benefactor of increasingly powerful but dependent trade unions. Perón committed Argentina to light industralization and used the power of the state to shield these enterprises from foreign competition.

When the post-World War II economy contracted, Perón modified his policies. The military and church leaders who had once supported him deserted the coalition, and the austerity policies he instituted alienated his popular base. By 1955, Perón was faced with two choices: arm his supporters to continue his policies of social reform or retreat from them into exile. He chose the latter.

Peronism did not resolve the economic future of the country, and subsequent governments foundered on the same obstacle. Nine successive governments, military and civilian, all but one elected or installed without the participation of the banned Peronist movement, sought to return Argentina to its agro-export past, to open the country to large infusions of foreign capital, or both. These two strategies shared certain characteristics. In particular, development was intended to occur at the expense of the working class. The inefficient entrepreneurs whom the Peronist state had protected were to be exposed to the competition of the free market, presumably to be driven out of business by multinational corporations.

The working class, still Peronist, was sufficiently strong to block, if not the introduction, at least the successful completion of these policies. In this way, Argentina's economic crisis was translated into a political stalemate with none of the factions powerful enough to impose its solution on the others. After 1955, Argentina began a period of prolonged stagnation and rising inflation. Inequalities in income distribution continued. The net effect of this deadlock was to radicalize a new generation, which looked either to one or another variation of Marxism or to a romanticized version of Peronism for solutions. Throughout the 1960s and 1970s more and more radical options proved unable to surmount Argentina's crisis.

THE JEWISH COMMUNITY IN 1945

Until 1945, at least, Jews did not experience in Argentina the same degree of mobility that Jews are assumed to have enjoyed in the United States. The Argentine economy was not sufficiently industrialized to generate those opportunities that stimulate mobility. The pattern of Argentine economic development, especially its limited and uneven industrial growth, placed important obstacles in the paths of the potentially mobile. The structural difficulties facing aspiring entrepreneurs were too much for most of them to overcome. Not until the Depression did successive governments support and protect the basic economic diversification necessary to help cushion the Argentine economy from the vagaries of international commerce.

As long as those who aspired to economic success were restrained by factors beyond their control, their hopes counted for little. Inflation, the high cost of living, constantly fluctuating demand, the absence of sufficiently protective tariffs, the reliance of domestic industry on foreign products, the expansiveness and frequent unavailability of raw materials, and the omnipresent threat of foreign competition made the position of both workers and owners precarious. Even the advent of import substitution coincided with the Depression to create new problems and worsen old ones.

Many workers saw self-employment as less desirable than wage earning, suggesting that self-employment in and of itself is not a totally accurate index of upward mobility. Data on business mortality also show the brittleness of these occupational changes and indicate that in many cases the shift from worker to owner was largely illusory. The phenomenon of skill displacement marginalized skilled workers, and the habituation of workers to those trades prevented shifts to the sectors of the economy that were expanding. Other restrictions, including anti-Semitism, also helped limit Jews to petty commerce.

The structural limitations on occupational mobility also influenced the shape and function of the community's institutions. The constant waves of immigration, infusions of workers seeking skilled and un-skilled jobs, and the insecure petty bourgeoisie kept the community's class structure in a state of flux. Because the Chevrah adhered to its original purposes, it remained open to workers (if not always demo-cratic) and never deteriorated to the point of being a booster society for the Jewish middle class. Residential concentration in ghettoes meant that newcomers could always be recruited easily, especially since east-ern European Jews were experienced joiners.[6] During the first half century of its existence, the Chevrah steadily expanded its functions and responsibilities, becoming the pre-eminent institution in the com-munity. In this it differed from the institutions that Jews in London and New York founded in an attempt to recreate the traditional Kehillah. What one historian called the "quest for community" failed in these cities. In Buenos Aires, in contrast, the Chevrah was successful, largely because of the community's lack of occupational and residen-tial mobility.

Until 1945, the Jews of Buenos Aires, like other immigrants to Argentina, may well have "nourish[ed] the illusion of being not only in a country as advanced as the one [they] had left, but in one with far more brilliant prospects." For most of them, however, social mobility and economic security remained an illusion.[7] The system was inflexi-ble, more rigid than scholars, for example, generally perceived. This rigidity was not without its social costs.

The restricted mobility of the Jewish community indicates that in 1946, the year of Perón's election to the presidency, Argentina was still a highly stratified society. Its leaders, civilian or military, believed Argentina's world role to be that of an exporter of beef and cereals, import substitution notwithstanding. Jews, like most Argentines, were on the margins of power.

Because active participation in electoral politics was limited to naturalized immigrants, few Jews voted. Successive regimes also placed obstacles in the paths of those foreigners who were willing to assume the responsibilities and privileges of Argentine citizenship. The political parties that offered the greatest prospects for mobility were those least likely to attract or to recruit working-class or petty bourgeois immigrants from eastern Europe. The oligarchy's conserva-tive parties held little for Jews, who were far removed from the export sector and from the class background required for admittance into the highest levels of Argentine society. Nor did radicalism's xenophobic appeals to the *criollo* middle class provide much encouragement, especially after the Tragic Week temporarily put an end to informal contacts between the community and the government. Unsuccessful efforts to establish independent political organizations suggest that segments of the Jewish working class was disaffected from the major parties, including the Socialists. The opposition of the Jewish community leadership to the strategy of the Jewish political party undoubtedly reinforced the alienation of the Jewish working class.

Even so, at least one Jew, Dr. Leopoldo Bard, a medical doctor who had been graduated from the University of Buenos Aires, rose through the ranks of the Radical party to become a national deputy. In this regard, he resembled Enrique Dickmann, a prominent member of the Socialist party and the first Jew to hold national office in Argentina. Dickmann's brother Adolfo also was a Socialist representative from Buenos Aires. In 1927, only one other Jew, Manuel D. Hartz, a police commissioner, merited mention as a Jew prominent in politics. All of these men were notable exceptions to the community's occupational preferences.[8]

Jewish participation in Argentine politics increased after Perón came to power. In 1961, a Jew became a recognized leader of the Conservative party. Also, as Radicalism became increasingly petty bourgeois, Jewish participation in the party's activities increased. Similarly, as the Socialist party lost its base in the working class and became a party of the petty bourgeoisie, Jews became more prominent in it, though the party became increasingly marginal. Between 1936 and 1951, Jews accounted for 14 percent of the leadership of the Socialist party.

Gauging other changes in the leadership of political parties after the election of Perón in 1946, José Luis de Imaz notes that "if to this we add that for the first time in the history of the country a Jew occupied the office of secretary with ministerial rank, we will have an idea of how social mobility worked up to that point in Argentina." After 1946, he continued, "conditions were created that, at the opportune political juncture, permitted a very significant percentage of the rulers to emerge from the lower social strata."[9]

Under Perón's industrialization policies, Jews finally began to approximate the mobility patterns of Jews in the United States. Among their other effects, these policies created a more solid Jewish middle class than had existed previously as well as a larger, self-made Jewish upper class.

While the Jewish community's leadership was often drawn from the ranks of the economically successful, Argentine culture as a whole chose to reward a different kind of accomplishment. The Argentine

Who's Who for 1939 and 1947 illustrate this distinction. Only ten eastern European Jews appeared among the 1,500 entries in 1939. Nine
were males, all of whom lived in Buenos Aires; one was an army
colonel, three were physicians, and six were authors. Five of them had
married non-Jews and four had married Jews. In 1947, there were
thirty-one Jews among 2,500 entries. Only two were active in trade or
industry; doctors, attorneys, engineers, and authors counted for 78
percent of the total. Of the twenty-six for whom there were marriage
data, fourteen had married Jews.[10]

As a rule, Jews regarded as prominent by Argentine society had
tenuous ties to the Jewish community. Only one of the thirty-one people included in the 1947 *Who's Who* appeared in a 1941 directory of
Jewish community leaders. That man, Boris Knobel, was a naturalized
Argentine of working-class parents who had become a textile indus-
trialist. At the same time, four of thirty Jews listed in a 1945 directory
of businessmen played important public roles in the community.[11]

The Argentine majority culture placed a priority on letters, the
law, and medicine. The Jewish community, on the other hand, more
frequently rewarded business acumen. Argentine Jews listed in *Who's
Who* had few contacts with the community, while the community leadership had few formal ties with Argentine society. That the community's leaders never countenanced intermarriage partially explains this
distance. Equally important is that recognition by the Argentine majority required, in addition to intelligence, luck, and diligence, adoption of
an ethos different from that esteemed by the community. While the
Chevrah recognized entrepreneurial success, Argentina rewarded less
material accomplishments.

THE JEWISH COMMUNITY SINCE WORLD WAR II

The rise, success, and staying power of Peronism over the course
of three decades, the apparent bankruptcy of traditional civilian politics, the frequent and increasingly brutal interventions of the military,
and an economic dilemma of epic proportions all played major parts in
shaping postwar Argentina and its Jewish community. Between
Perón's election in 1946 and his death in 1974, the Jewish community of
Buenos Aires changed in certain ways and remained static in others.
Most notably, by March 1976, when the military most recently intervened in politics, the ability of the community's institutions to satisfy
its members' needs and defend them from harm was severely circumscribed.

The heightened social consciousness of the postwar Argentine state enabled it to provide more benefits than could the Chevrah, and membership in the Chevrah declined. Postwar occupational mobility, increased geographic dispersion, acculturation, assimilation, and especially intermarriage have reduced the number of Jews available for membership. In addition, many thousands of Jews have chosen to leave Argentina.

Although the Chevrah, renamed the Asociación Mutual Israelita Argentina (AMIA) in 1941, remains the largest Jewish voluntary association in Argentina, its demographic profile is not encouraging. Almost 95 percent of the members are now first-generation Argentines, more than 70 percent of them over fifty years old. More than half are over sixty years of age and need more services while being less able to pay for them. Maintaining membership and recruitment are continuing problems. In 1976, more than 8,500 members either did not pay dues or left the association, while only 756 new members joined in the first ten months of 1977. The community's funds still come mainly from funerals, but increasingly Jews are buried elsewhere, depriving the AMIA of much needed income.[12] Inflation, which has run rampant in Argentina for the last decade, has also been cheapening its remaining assets.

Younger Jews have found a number of ways to show their displeasure and alienation from the community. A 1966 study undertaken by the Delegación de Asociaciones Israelitas Argentina (DAIA), the community's umbrella defense organization, found that of some 90,000 youths between the ages of ten and twenty-five, only 38 percent were affiliated with a Jewish institution. The majority belonged to sports clubs and the like, which the DAIA said had no "Jewish content." Less than 10 percent of those questioned belonged to an organization active in specifically Jewish concerns. The others either claimed allegiance to political parties or movements or advocated assimilation. Of the approximately 17,000 Jewish university students, representing 3.4 percent of the total Jewish population, only 8 percent were active in Jewish affairs of one kind or another.[13]

The wave of political radicalism that swept Latin America after the Cuban revolution did not miss Argentina. The belief that the country was "dependent," and that radical solutions were needed to reverse the "development of underdevelopment," politicized Argentine society, especially its universities. Over at least the last two decades Jews have comprised more than 16 percent of the university population, and a high percentage of them were active in student politics. Because Argentine society and politics is class based and lacks a tradition of cultural pluralism and because the community has so little to offer them, most Jewish students have chosen to be active in national rather than community matters. There is no tradition in Argentina, such as exists in the United States, of the two being compatible. By 1971, only 5.8 percent of the Jewish university students belonged to a Jewish organization, and only about 4 percent belonged to a Zionist organization.[14]

The community is in no position to remedy the situation by reaching Jewish children of elementary school age. The Jewish educational system, which is increasingly expensive to maintain, does not attract a significant percentage of the total Jewish population. Most of the 15 percent who do attend such schools are clustered in the lower grades and drop out after three years. Frequently, teachers leave because of low salaries. The net result is that a new generation is growing up ignorant of its past.

In 1967, a government decree that all school children had to attend both morning and afternoon sessions eliminated afternoon instruction, forcing the Jewish community to spend large sums on day schools offering both secular and religious courses. Jewish cooperative associations, which had been an important source of financial support for the school system, were nationalized during the regime of President Alejandro Lanusse (1971–73), depriving the schools of their contributions. Only infusions of capital from abroad have kept the school system afloat.[15] Shocks to the school system continued to plague the community in the mid-1970s. In August 1975, teachers struck for higher wages, reminiscent of an earlier strike more than half a century earlier. Yitzhok Korn, Secretary General of the Avodah or Labor party in Israel, was disturbed "by the undefinable indifference of the vast majority of Argentine Jews to the local emergency and its consequences on Jewish education." He said more recently that "now we are talking of the possible collapse of the entire educational system."[16]

It is an oversimplification to attribute the community's internal crisis to politically radical youth or to the failure of the school system to properly educate youngsters. Their parents have also demonstrated dissatisfaction with the community in a variety of ways.

In the aftermath of a particularly disappointing turnout in community elections in 1969, the AMIA leadership tried to discern the reasons for voter apathy. More than 46 percent of those polled responded that the election simply held no interest for them, 39 percent claimed to have been away from Buenos Aires or otherwise indisposed, and 9 percent expressed doubts about the administration of the community's affairs. Presumably, if they cared about the election, many of the 39 percent would have modified their plans and been in Buenos Aires to vote on the appointed day. It certainly appears that far more than half of the membership is indifferent to the well-publicized election campaigns.[17]

A fundamental problem facing the community's institutions is that Jews of all ages and political persuasions believe that the institutions have become irrelevant. In recent AMIA elections, according to the newspaper *Mundo Israelita* (Jewish World), "of the 46,000 members, only 34,000 were in voting condition, and of those only 7,811 [17 percent] voted."[18] In 1968, the AMIA counted 46,304 voting members. There has been no real growth in membership in the last decade.

Another symptom of the internal malaise is intermarriage in the community. Accurate data are lacking, but it is a significant problem affecting perhaps one-quarter of those marrying. The records of the Chevrah indicate that the problem is not a new one. Jews in Buenos Aires were intermarrying fifty years ago, although the implication is that intermarriage was more prevalent among well-to-do families. While the Chevrah never admitted families composed of only one Jewish partner, it occasionally did bury the Jewish spouse. By the mid-1920s, opposition to this policy was hardening, but no firm guidelines for a coherent policy could be agreed upon, because "not all cases arise in the same form or in the same social spheres" and because some of the families in question enjoyed special relationships to the leadership. The issue was discussed again in 1930 because the phenomenon had become more widespread and because one faction believed that a more tolerant attitude toward intermarriage was needed. The Orthodox members, who argued that a Jewish wedding was a minimal prerequisite for membership, prevailed.[19]

The changing attitudes of much of the Jewish community since World War II arose in the context of greater occupational mobility than ever before. According to one observer,

> a very significant tendency towards a change in the economic activity of the Jews since the Second World War should be noted. Many companies which dealt only in the purchase of raw materials or primary products and their resale in the original form, decided to undertake their processing and improvement; at first . . . in open competition and finally in confrontation with the goods of the traditional suppliers from abroad. The Jewish cloth importer began to manufacture cloth in Argentina itself. This phenomenon spread to many and varied goods—from parts of radio sets and telephones, through construction goods to various spare parts and accessories for automobiles. In export branches too, the sellers of raw hides began to sell them after tanning and cutting and export of furs as a raw material ended up in the manufacture of finished products.[20]

A 1962 survey of some 1,700 Jewish couples married in synagogues in Buenos Aires indicates more precisely the effect of these changes. Where 15 percent of the parents were workers, only 6 percent of the younger generation were. Almost half of the parents earned livelihoods derived from commerce, but only a third of the children did. Four times as many children (25 percent) as parents belonged to the professional class. Finally, 16 percent of the children, as compared to 6 percent of the parents, were officials. A second study commissioned in the early 1960s determined that 95.5 percent of the organized eastern European Jewish community was "middle class" and 3.5 percent was working class.[21] These studies no doubt reflect a liberal interpretation of class and status, but Jews certainly experienced greater mobility after 1945 than before.

Determining how accurate these statistics are would require another in-depth sampling, but other sources, easier to compile, indicate that they are optimistic and misleading. By the mid-1960s, for example, the Joint Distribution Committee, a worldwide Jewish relief organization, had stopped sending immigrants to Argentina because of the lack of economic opportunity. Economic stagnation also stimulated out-migration from Argentina. Between June 1962 and May 1963, about 2,000 Jews, most of them professionals, technicians, and university graduates, emigrated to the United States. About 5,000 chose to go to Israel.[22] Still another example of the community's uneven economic picture is that some 6,200 people applied to the AMIA for financial assistance in the first half of 1970.[23]

These problems within the Jewish community have certainly been exacerbated by the policies of the current government, but they antedate the 1976 coup d'état in which it came to power. Within certain sectors of the community, this unpleasant fact of life has been a matter of much concern. *Mundo Israelita* editorialized that:

> We must, once and for all, state unequivocally that the main problem is the frightening disappearance of Jewish content and feeling, which is a common denominator of the vast majority of our Jews. This basic lack of Jewish identification is responsible to a far greater extent for our crisis than is the devouring inflationary-recessionary economic crisis. It is high time that we freely confess that Argentine Jews could cover their own expenses if they were properly organized and committed. Besides the lack of Jewish values and voluntary spirit, we must also confront the vicious image of an antiquated an obsolete community structure.[24]

As the present political crisis deepens, the community, suffering from the alienation of its members, from reduced income, and from a population decline of perhaps 100,000 in the past decade, becomes increasingly less able to confront its problems and meet its needs. In an unfortunate confluence of historical developments, the community is weakest precisely when the forces of reaction are strongest.

RECENT ANTI-SEMITISM

There are several explanations for the virulence of the anti-Semitism that has recently gripped Argentina, but all of them are unsatisfactory to the historian. For example, Argentina's Catholic tradition, agitation by those Nazis who entered the country in the 1940s, and Arab propaganda have all been blamed for the latest upsurge in anti-Jewish activity. Argentina, however, is not a Catholic country by any standard except nominal attachment, and Argentine anti-Semitism predates both the Second World War and Arab-Israeli hostility.

The history of Argentine anti-Semitism suggests that such prejudice has always been strongest among adherents of the nationalist right and that the Jewish community has never combated these forces effectively. A 1961 report by Argentine sociologist Gino Germani revealed that 22.1 percent of the Argentine population harbored anti-Semitic attitudes. While the percentage of anti-Semites rose as one descended the social scale, Germani nevertheless concluded that upper-class anti-Semitism was more dangerous because it was "ideological" rather than traditional. A similar study, which arrived at similar percentages, included a survey of sixty military officers, almost 75 percent of whom were anti-Semitic. Results of still another survey, conducted in 1967 after four years of intense anti-Semitic agitation, found that almost 40 percent of the population was anti-Semitic, but that the upper class was more anti-Semitic still.[25]

The depth of this anti-Semitism was graphically spelled out in Jacobo Timerman's memoir of his arrest and torture by elements of the Argentine military. According to Timerman, "the military examiners or police felt toward left-wing terrorists the way you might feel toward an enemy. These political prisoners were not spared when it came to torture or murder, but the psychological relationship was simple—confrontation with one's enemy. With Jews, however, there was a desire to eradicate wholesale."[26]

Timerman reported that "the Jewish question dominated every interrogation, during my entire imprisonment." No response could satisfy his torturers. "Thus, I was never able to prove to my interrogators that Zbigniew Brzezinski was not a Jew and not the head of a

Latin-American Jewish conspiracy, or that Sol Linowitz, the former United States Ambassador to the Organization of American States, was not second-in-command to Brzezinski and I not his Argentine representative. Some things cannot be proved."[27]

These surveys, and Timerman's recollections, suggest a continuous current of anti-Semitism that rises after agitation and economic decline or stagnation. They also demonstrate the volatility of the issue and how anti-Semitism can be manipulated by those at the top of the social scale to inflame the passions of those at the bottom. "Ideological" anti-Semitism, it seems, has never taken root in the Argentine middle or working classes.

The wave of anti-Semitism in 1978 is at least partially attributable to the accession to power of a group of already anti-Semitic military men who represent an Argentine elite that much prefers authoritarianism to democracy. Contemporary anti-Semitism can best be understood as part of the country's larger political and economic crises. For the last five years at least, Argentina has been in the throes of a *de facto* civil war between the revolutionary left, especially Peronist and Marxist guerrilla organizations, and the reactionary right well represented in the military. The roots of this war lie in Argentina's inability to achieve a consensus on that decades-old-issue—whether its economy should emphasize the agro-export market or industrialization.

Perhaps the single most important even in the radicalization of this conflict was the *Cordobazo,* a more or less spontaneous uprising of workers and students in Córdoba, Argentina's most radical city, in 1969. The violence exposed the weakness of what was the strictest military government Argentina had ever endured, soon toppling it. From this heady experience arose left-wing guerrilla groups such as the Peronist Montoneros. By 1972, having demonstrated its ability to mobilize large numbers of people in popular demonstrations, the left seemed to be in control of a revived Peronist movement.

Left-wing Peronists, guerrillas, and trade unionists alike, assumed that Perón shared their aspirations for national liberation and socialism. Simultaneously, the military, the traditional elite, and the Peronist right perceived Perón as the last defense against the left. Although hostility between the left and the right wings of the movement increased, Perón, who had returned to Argentina after eighteen years of exile to be elected president for the third time in 1973, successfully managed the conflict.

His widow and successor, María Isabel de Perón or "Isabelita" as she is known, lacked her husband's skills, and after Perón's death in July 1974 the two wings of the Peronist movement went to war. Out of this internecine struggle for power came the violence that still characterizes Argentina.

In the twenty-one months that she ruled Argentina, Isabel Perón presided over the further deterioration of the Peronist movement and the worsening of the country's economic difficulties. Inflation, at 700 percent a year, was probably the worst in the world. Wage freezes exacerbated the plight of the working class and other wage earners; import restrictions hurt the private sector; and violence became endemic.

As the crisis deepened, certain facts emerged. The struggle for power took place within the Peronist movement because other civilian political parties proved unable to strike sympathetic chords among the populace. When the military intervened, it did so in opposition to the corruption and misrule of the Peronist right, although its campaign against the left revealed no sympathy for it. In fact, the military had already been fighting the guerrillas for control of the state well before the coup.

In addition to the usual right-wing myths and stereotypes, the role of prominent Jews in the economy (an aspect of ideological anti-Semitism) motivates the regime's anti-Jewish attitudes. Entrepreneurs such as Jacobo Timerman, former publisher of the newspaper *La Opinión,* David Gravier, a deceased Jewish financier, and Julio Broner and José Ber Gelbard, both former heads of the CGE, were prominent members of the national bourgeoisie, allied to varying degrees with sectors of the Peronist movement. They made convenient targets in the attack against the Peronists. Also, the visibility of young Jews in university politics and in left-wing movements called attention to the entire community. Finally, there are in the present government men who quite simply *believe* anti-Semitic myths and stereotypes, men who are now in positions of power where they can act on these prejudices.

The community has responded to this latest crisis in traditional ways. The DAIA has agreed with the junta that "our country . . . is not an anti-Semitic country, nor does official anti-Semitism exist." It has argued that blame should be laid at the door of "the groups of real economic power who use it [anti-Semitism] to hide their own enormous responsibility for the country's problems." The DAIA announced its intention "to try to work with the more representative figures of the national government," but called attention to the "dark and pogromist forces" at work in Argentina today. It warned that "there no longer exist passive and silent Jewish masses" but gave no indication of what it meant to imply.[28]

The community's responses are consistent with the positions it adopted during the two previous periods of intense anti-Semitic activity in 1919 and 1943, when the leadership sought to influence matters informally, implicitly accepting some of the anti-Semites' allegations. The community has never tried to test its strength against anti-Semitic threats. Instead, it has presumed its own weakness and proceeded with the utmost caution.

At this writing, anti-Semitic agitation has subsided. But the violence of the past few years can reappear at any time. If it is to stem the tide of anti-Semitism and revitalize itself, the organized Jewish community of Buenos Aires must confront the effects of long-term structural crises; it must recognize the consequences of reacting too slowly and too ineffectively to major problems within the community as well as outside it. Indeed, it is this crisis—the crisis of community in an advanced stage—that magnifies the impact of anti-Semitic activities. Each onslaught shows the community to be weaker than before and therefore less likely to resist the next time around.

More than three-quarters of a century has elapsed since the first Russian Jewish immigrants disembarked from the steamship *Weser* at Buenos Aires. In the succeeding decades much has happened to their children and grandchildren. In many ways, some of them subtle and many of them obvious, these descendants have also left their mark on Argentine society and politics.

As we have seen, their experiences are too varied to permit facile summations and judgments. Argentina has been kind to many Jews and unkind to others; at times, it has been both. While anti-Semitism has lingered and has, at times, become virulent, we cannot compare anti-Semitism in Argentina to either the random violence of the Russian pogrom or to the systematic genocide of Hitler's Germany.

We cannot judge, in the final analysis, whether Jewish immigrants expected more from Argentina than they received. All that is clear is that the journey from Pale to Pampa and the subsequent efforts to establish a viable community were fraught with difficulties that tried the resources that community had at its disposal. In that sense, perhaps, Argentina proved to be no different from other countries.

Notes

1. *American Jewish Year Book,* vol. 48, 1946–1947, p. 248.
2. José Luis de Imaz, *Los que mandan* translated by Carlos A. Astiz (Albany: State University of New York Press, 1970) p. 138.

3. *American Jewish Year Book,* vol. 50, 1948–1949, p. 269.

4. Juan José Sebreli, *La cuestion judía en la Argentina* (Buenos Aires: Editorial Tiempo Contemporaneo), p. 156.

5. Natan Lerner, "Anti-Semitism and the Nationalist Ideology in Argentina," *Dispersion and Unity,* 17–18 (1973) and David Stephen, "The Radical Right in Latin America," *Wiener Library Bulletin,* 22 (Spring 1968), pp. 25–30.

6. Unfortunately, precise information about the membership patterns of Jewish immigrants in other associations was hard to come by. All sample members were traced, with varying degrees of success, through the partial records of almost one hundred voluntary, commercial, religious, and political organizations. Fragmentary data revealed only five members each in Samples 2 and 3, and only two in Sample 5, who joined other associations. The more complete data offered by the 1920 and 1925 samples indicate, however, that Jews enrolled in associations other than the Chevrah in impressive numbers. In the former sample 130 men, or 46.8 percent, were members of other organizations when they began to pay dues to the Chevrah. Five years later, 79 or 28.4 percent reported their affiliation with other associations. Incomplete data for the 1895 cohort indicate that at least 11.4 percent of those who eventually joined the Chevrah Keduscha also belonged to other voluntary associations. This situation is attributable to a desire to maintain ethnic cohesiveness in the face of real, or potential, adversity and to the passive function that the Argentine oligarchy assigned to the State. Government undertook little or no responsibility for the care and welfare of its citizens; instead, voluntary associations met those needs.

7. José Luis Romero, *El desarollo de las ideas en la sociedad argentina del siglo XX* (Mexico-Buenos Aires: Fondo de Cultura Económica, 1965), p. 9.

8. Adolfo Segall, ed., *Anuario Israelita,* 1926–1927 (Buenos Aires: Segall y Capellano Hnos, 1927), pp. LI–LIII.

9. José Luis de Imaz, *Los que mandan,* pp. 202 and 19.

10. *Quien es quien en la Argentina; Primer edición* (Buenos Aires: Guillermo Kraft, Ltda. 1939) and *Quien es quien en la Argentina; Cuarta edición* (Buenos Aires: Guillermo Kraft, Ltda. 1947).

11. Wolf Bresler y Samuel Glasserman, *Lexicon de los hombres de bien de la colectividad israelita en la Argentina* (Buenos Aires: Tall. Graf. Cultura, 1941), p. 198 and *Hombres de la Argentina, Diccionario biografico contemporáneo,* segunda edición, 1946 (Buenos Aires: Veritas, 1946).

12. *American Jewish Year Book,* vol. 77, 1977, p. 340.

13. Ibid., vol. 68, 1967, p. 270.

14. Bernardo Kligsberg, "La juventud judía en la Argentina," *Nueva Zion* (September 1971), 7.

15. Robert Weisbrot, "Jews in Argentina Today," *Judaism* 25 (Fall 1976), 391.

16. *American Jewish Year Book,* vol. 77, 1977, pp. 343–344.

17. Teresa Kaplanski de Caryevschi, *Características de los socios de la AMIA* (Buenos Aires: Instituto de Investigaciones Sociales, 1970), pp. 17 and 34.

18. *American Jewish Year Book,* vol. 77, 1977, p. 341.

19. Chevrah Keduscha, *Minutes,* August 29, 1926 and July 20, 1930.

20. *See:* Abraham Scheps, *El aporte judío en la economia Argentina* (Buenos Aires: Primera Conferencia de Investigadores y Estudiosos, 1961).

21. A. Monk and E. Rogovsky, *Survey,* quoted in Haim Avni, "Argentina Jewry: Its Social Position and Organizational Patterns," *Dispersion and Unity* 12–13 (1971), p. 147.
22. *American Jewish Year Book,* vol. 65, 1964, p. 178.
23. *Kehillah,* vol. I, (1971), p. 9.
24. *American Jewish Year Book,* vol. 77, 1977, p. 342.
25. Robert Weisbrot, "Antisemitism in Argentina," *Midstream* 24 (May 1978), 17 and 23.
26. Jacobo Timerman, "No Name, No Number," *The New Yorker,* April 20, 1981, p. 96.
27. Ibid., p. 101.
28. Quotation, Eugene F. Sofer, "Argentine Jewry: What We Need to Know," *Interchange* 1 (1977).

BIBLIOGRAPHY

I. ARCHIVES

Archivo General de la Nación, Buenos Aires
Archivo de Tribunales, Buenos Aires
Associación Mutual Israelita Argentina (AMIA), Buenos Aires
Yiddisher Wisnshaftlecher Institut Archives (IWO), Buenos Aires

II. QUANTITATIVE SOURCES

Asilo Israelita Argentina para ancianos y huérfanos. *Anuario con la primera guía israelita en la República Argentina*. Buenos Aires, 1921.

———. *Anuario y guía israelita en la República Argentina*. Buenos Aires, 1923.

Guía Anual Israelita, 1945. Buenos Aires, 1945.

República Argentina. *Segundo Censo Nacional* (vol. 466–656). Manuscript in the possession of the Archivo General de la Nación, Buenos Aires.

———. *Segundo censo de la República Argentina*. Tomos I–III. Buenos Aires, 1898.

———. *Censo General de Población, Edificación, Comercio e Industrias de la Ciudad de Buenos Aires, 1904*. Buenos Aires, 1906.

———. *Censo General de Población, Edificación, Comercio e Industrias de la Ciudad de Buenos Aires, 1909*. Buenos Aires, 1910.

———. *Tercer Censo Nacional, 1914*. Buenos Aires, 1916.

———. *Censo Industrial de 1935*. Buenos Aires, 1938.

———. *Cuarto Censo General de la Nación, 1947*. Buenos Aires, 1947.

Segall, Adolfo, ed. *Anuario Israelita, 1926–1927*. Buenos Aires, 1927.

Unión Telefónica. *Capital Federal y suburbios, 1907*. Buenos Aires, 1907.

———. *Capital Federal y suburbios, 1917*. Buenos Aires, 1917.

———. *Capital Federal y suburbios, 1936*. Buenos Aires, 1936.

III. SOURCES FROM THE ASOCIACIÓN MUTUAL ISRAELITA ARGENTINA

Libros de Actas, vols. I–VIII, 1895–1936.
Registros de Socios, 1895–1945.
Sepelios, 1917–1973, vols. 1–574; 1–94.
Solicitudes, 1920–1935, vols. 1–31; 1B–30B; 1C–7C.

IV. VOLUNTARY ASSOCIATION MEMBERSHIP LISTS

Anglo-Jewish Association, 1897–1904.
Asociación Israelita Religiosa, 1941–42.
Asociación Juventud Israelita Argentina, 1916.
Centro Estudiantil Hebreo, 1913.
Comisión Israelita Pro–Centenario, 1910.
Comisión Pro–Monumento Israelita (and subscription list).
Comité Hebreo, 1913.
Comité Pro–Víctimas de Marruecos, 1912.
Congregación Israelita, 1943–1945.
Cooperativa Comercial Israelita, 1916 and 1924.
Corporación Comercial Israelita Argentina, 1929.
Der Jugend, 1908.
Federación Israelita Argentina, 1909.
Sholem Aleichem Folk Schule, 1921–1922.
Sociedad "Chovevi Zion," 1897.
Sociedad Ezrah, 1913.
Sociedad Israelita "Gmilath Jasodim" de Parque Patricios, 1918.
Sociedad "La Unión Obrera Israelita," 1898.
Tesoro Israelita Argentina, 1911.

V. BANKS AND CREDIT INSTITUTIONS

Banco Comercial, 1936–1939.
Banco de Buenos Aires, 1931; 1934–1938.
Banco de Liniers
Banco de Villa Crespo, 1935–1936.
Banco Industrial, 1934–1946.
Banco Israelita Argentina, 1923–1938.

Banco Israelita de Crédito, 1924–1939.
Banco Israelita del Río de la Plata, 1940–1942.
Banco Israelita Polaco, 1935–1938.
Banco Mercantil Argentino, 1940–1947.
Caja Comercial de Crédito, 1935 and 1938.
Primera Caja Mercantil, 1941–1943.

VI. BUENOS AIRES

Buénos Aires. *Annuaire Statistique de la Ville de Buénos Ayres, 1900*. Buénos Ayres, 1900.

———. *Digesto Municipal de la Ciudad de Buenos Aires*. Buenos Aires, 1938.

———. *Proyecto orgánico para la urbanización del municipio*. Buenos Aires, 1925.

VII. UNITED STATES

Rubinow, I. M. "Economic Condition of the Jews in Russia." *Bulletin of the United States Bureau of Labor* XV (September 1907), 487–583.

United States. Bureau of Labor Statistics. *Monthly Labor Review*, 1902–1950.

———. Department of Commerce. *Shoe and Leather Trade in Argentina, Chile, Peru, and Uruguay*. Washington, D.C. Government Printing Office, 1910.

———. Department of Commerce. *Wearing Apparel in Argentina*. Washington, D.C. Government Printing Office, 1918.

———. Department of Commerce. *Boots and Shoes, Leather, and Supplies in Argentina, Uruguay, and Paraguay*. Washington D.C. Government Printing Office, 1919.

———. Department of Commerce. *Furniture Markets of Argentina, Uruguay, and Brazil*. Washington, D.C. Government Printing Office, 1919.

———. Department of Commerce, *Advertising Methods in Argentina, Uruguay and Brazil*. Washington, D.C. Government Printing Office, 1920.

———. Department of Commerce. *The Economic Position of Argentina During the War*. Washington, D.C. Government Printing Office, 1920.

———. Department of Commerce. *Textile Markets of Argentina, Uruguay, and Paraguay*. Washington, D.C. Government Printing Office, 1920.

———. Department of Commerce. *Jewelry and Silverware in Argentina, Uruguay, and Brazil*. Washington, D.C. Government Printing Office, 1922.

———. Department of Commerce. *Textile Market of Argentina*. Washington, D.C. Government Printing Office, 1932.

————. House of Representatives. *Executive Documents for the Fifty-Second Congress, 1891–1892.* vol. I. Washington, D.C. Government Printing Office, 1892.

————. United States Senate. 76th Congress. 3rd Session. Investigation of Concentration of Economic Power. *Technology in Our Economy.* Washington, D.C. Government Printing Office, 1941.

VIII. GREAT BRITAIN

Great Britain. *Report on the Financial, Commercial, and Economic Conditions of the Argentina Republic, September, 1925.* London: H. M. Stationery Office, 1925.

————. Department of Overseas Trade, *Economic Conditions in the Argentine Republic.* November 1929–June 1937. London: H. M. Stationery Office, 1929–1937.

IX. SPECIAL REPORTS

American Committee on the Rights of Religious Minorities. *Roumania: Ten Years After.* Boston: Beacon Press, 1928.

Cámara Argentina de la Construcción, *El problema de la vivienda.* Buenos Aires: Cámara Argentina de la Construcción, 1950.

Comité Argentino de Moralidad Pública y Contra la Trata de Blancas. *Estatuos y reglamento.* Buenos Aires: Comite Argentino de Moralidad Publica, etc., 1909.

Comité de la Colectividad Israelita. *Exposición de atropellos contra instituciones e individuos de la colectividad Israelita.* Buenos Aires: Comite de la Colectividad, 1919.

Confederación Argentina de Industrias Textiles. *La industria textil argentina.* Buenos Aires: Confederación Argentina de Industrias Textiles, 1934.

"Di Presse," *Cincuenta años de la vida judía en el país; XX aniversario de "Di Presse,"* Buenos Aires: "Di Presse," 1938.

Joint Foreign Committee of the Board of Deputies of British Jews and the Anglo Jewish Association. *The Jewish Minority in Roumania.* London: Joint Foreign Committee of the Board of Deputies, etc., 1927.

National Polish Committee of America. *The Jews in Poland.* Chicago: National Polish Committee of America, n.d.

Rapoport, Nicolás, ed. *Libro del cincuentenario de la Ezrah y Hospital Israelita.* Buenos Aires: Talleres Gráficos Julio Kaufman, 1950.

República Argentina. Departamento Nacional del Trabajo. *Boletín.* vols. 1–37. Buenos Aires: Departmento Nacional del Trabajo, 1907–1918.

———. Senado de la Nación. *Represión del comunismo*. II tomos. Buenos Aires: Imprenta del Congreso Nacional, 1936.

Sociedad Comercial e Industrial Israelita. S.A. *45 Aniversario*. Buenos Aires: Sociedad Comercial e Industrial Israelita, 1961.

Tiempo, Cesar, (psued.) *La campaña antisemita y el Director de la Biblioteca Nacional*. Buenos Aires: Ediciones DAIA, 1935.

Triwaks, Hirsch, ed. *Cincuenta años de vida judía en la Argentina*. Buenos Aires: Talleres Graficos Julio Kaufman, 1940.

Weill, Simon. *Población israelita en la República Argentina*. Buenos Aires: Bene Berith, 1936.

X. BIOGRAPHICAL DICTIONARIES

Bresler, Wolf and Samuel Glasserman, eds. *Lexicon de los hombres de bien de la colectividad israelita en la Argentina*. Buenos Aires: Tall. Graf. Cultura, 1941.

Diccionario biográfico de hombres de negocio. Buenos Aires: Veritas, 1945.

Diccionario biográfico contemporaneo. Buenos Aires: Veritas, 1946.

Quien es quien en la Argentina, primera edición. Buenos Aires: Guillermo Kraft, Ltda., 1939.

Quien es quien en la Argentina, cuarta edición. Buenos Ares: Guillermo Kraft, Ltda., 1947.

XI. UNPUBLISHED MANUSCRIPTS

Ansel, Bernard D. "The Beginnings of the Modern Jewish Community in Argentina, 1852–1891." doctoral dissertation. University of Kansas, 1970.

Dolkart, Ronald H. "Manuel A. Fresco, Governor of the Province of Buenos Aires, 1936–1940." doctoral dissertation. UCLA, 1969.

Gerassi, Marysa. "Argentine Nationalism of the Right." doctoral dissertation. Columbia University, 1964.

Herbert, J. R. "The Tragic Week of January, 1919 in Buenos Aires." doctoral dissertation. Georgetown University, 1972.

Hernando, Diana. "Casa y familia." doctoral dissertation. UCLA, 1973.

Hollander, Nancy Caro. "Women in the Political Economy of Argentina." doctoral dissertation. UCLA, 1974.

Kahan, Arcadius. "The Impact of the Industrialization Process in Tsarist Russia Upon the Socio-Economic Conditions of the Jewish Population (Observations and Comments)." paper. 1972.

Little, Walter. "Political Integration in Peronist Argentina." doctoral dissertation. Cambridge University. 1971.

Mirelman, Victor. "The Jews in Argentina (1890–1930): Assimilation and Particularism." doctoral dissertation. Columbia University, 1937.

Raczynski, Dagmar. "Occupational Mobility and Occupational Achievement in Santiago de Chile." doctoral dissertation. UCLA, 1970.

Rock, David. "Radicalism and the Urban Working Class in Argentina, 1916–1922." doctoral dissertation. Cambridge University, 1971.

Rubel, Yacov, "La década del 80 en la inmigración judía a la República Argentina." manuscript. Buenos Aires, 1972.

Sofer, Eugene F. and Mark D. Szuchman, "Opportunities for Quantitative Social History in Argentina Since 1869," paper. forthcoming.

Spalding, Hobart A. "Aspects of Change in Argentina, 1880–1914." doctoral dissertation. University of California, Berkeley, 1965.

Szuchman, Mark D. "Mobility and Integration in Urban Argentina: Córdoba in the Liberal Era." doctoral dissertation. University of Texas, 1975.

Tulchin, Joseph. "Agricultural Credit and Politics in Argentina, 1910–1922." paper. n.d.

Yans-McLaughlin, Virginia. "Like the Fingers of the Hand: The Family and Community Life of First Generation Italian-Americans in Buffalo, New York, 1890–1930," doctoral dissertation. State University of New York, Buffalo, 1970.

XII. PERIODICALS

American Jewish Year Book. 1940–1978.

Anuario *La Nación*. 1891.

C.G.T. (Confederación General de Trabajo), 1937.

Jewish Chronicle. 1887.

Juventud. 1911–1916.

Kehillah. 1970.

Las Bases. 1974.

London Daily Graphic. 1894.

Mayoría. 1973.

XIII. PRINTED SOURCES

Abad de Santillan, Diego. *La FORA*. 2nd ed. Buenos Aires: *Editorial Proyeccion, 1971*.

Abramovitch, Hirsch. "Rural Jewish Occupations in Lithuania." *YIVO Annual of Jewish Social Science* II–III (1948): 205–221.

Alder, Cyrus, ed. *The Voice of America on Kishineff.* Philadelphia: Jewish Publication Society of América, 1904.

—— and Aaron M. Margalith. *American Intercession on Behalf of Jews in the Diplomatic Correspondence of the United States, 1840–1938.* New York: American Jewish Historical Society, 1943.

Aitkin, Hugh G. J., ed. *Explorations in Enterprise.* Cambridge: Harvard University Press, 1967.

Akers, C. E. *Argentine, Patagonian, and Chilian Sketches.* London: Harrison and Sons, 1893.

Alsina, Juan A. *La immigración europea en la República Argentina.* Buenos Aires: Imprenta Calle México, 1898.

Alsogaray, Julio L. *Trilogía de la trata de blancas.* Buenos Aires: L. J. Rosso, 1933.

Ansel, Bernard A. "Discord Among Western and Eastern European Jews in Argentina." *American Jewish Historical Quarterly* LX (December 1970): 151–158.

Aronsfeld, C. C. "Jewish Bankers and the Tsar." *Jewish Social Studies* XXXV (April 1973): 87–104.

Avni, Haim. "Argentine Jewry: Its Social Position and Organization." pts. I and II, *Dispersion and Unity* 12–13 (1971): 128–162, 161–208.

——. "Argentine Jewry: Its Social Political Status and Organizational Patterns." pt. III, *Dispersion and Unity* 15–16 (1972): 158–215.

Babini, Nicolás. "La Semana Trágica." *Todo es Historia* I (September 1967): 8–23.

Babson, Roger W. *The Future of South America.* Boston: Little, Brown & Co., 1916.

Bagú, Sergio. *Evolución historica de la estratificación social en la Argentina.* Caracas: Esquima, 1969.

Baily, Samuel L. *Labor, Nationalism, and Politics in Argentina.* New Brunswick: Rutgers University Press, 1967.

Barager, Joseph. "The Historiography of the Río de la Plata Area Since 1830," *Hispanic American Historical Review* XXXIX (1959): 588–642.

Barnett, George E. *Chapters on Machinery and Labor.* Carbondale: Southern Illinois University Press, 1969.

Barres, M. *Males sociales: usureros.* Buenos Aires: Imprenta Lopez, 1939.

Bavio, Ernesto A. "Las escuelas extranjeras en Entre Ríos." *El monitor de educación común* XXVII–XXVIII (November 1908 and January 1909): 597–604 and 3–44.

Bayer, Osvaldo. "Simon Radowitzky, mártir o asesino?" *Todo es Historia* I (August 1967): 58–79.

Bechhofer, Frank and Brian Elliot. "An Approach to a Study of Small Shopkeepers and the Class Structure." *Archives Europeénes de Sociologie* IX (1968): 180–202.

Benario, M. "El comercio y la industria judíos en Buenos Aires." El Diario Israelita. *Homenaje a "El Diario Israelita."* 1940, pp. 75–76.

Bernstein, Barton, ed. *Towards A New Past.* New York: Vintage, 1968.

Bessero, Victorio L. *Los tratantes de blancas en Buenos Aires.* Buenos Aires: Editorial Aspansia, 1930.

Beyhaut, Gustavo, et al., "Los inmigrantes en el sistema occupacional argentino." In *Argentina: sociedad de masas,* edited by Torcuato Di Tella et al., 1965, pp. 85–123.

Bloch, Marc, "Toward A Comparative History of European Societies." In *Enterprise and Secular Change,* edited by Frederic C. Lane and Jellie C. Riemersma, pp. 489–493. Homewood: Richard D. Irwin, 1953.

Booth, Charles. *Life and Labour of the People in London.* vol. 4. London: Macmillan and Co., 1892.

Bourne, Larry S., ed. *Internal Structure of the City.* New York: Oxford University Press, 1972.

Broom, Leonard and F. Lancaster Jones. "Career Mobility in Three Societies: Australia, Italy, and the United States." *American Sociological Review,* 34 (October 1969): 650–658.

Brusilovsky, H. "Los judíos en el movimiento obrero argentino." El Diario Israelita. *Homenaje a "El Diario Israelita."* 1940, pp. 97–98.

Bryce, James. *South America.* New York: Macmillan and Co., 1912.

Bunge, Alejandro E. *Los problemas económicos del presente.* Buenos Aires: n.p., 1920.

———. *Una nueva argentina.* Buenos Aires: Editorial Kraft, 1940.

Bunge, Carlos O. *El espiritu de la educación.* Buenos Aires: n.p., 1901.

Burgess, Ernest W. "Residential Segregation in American Cities." *Annals of the American Academy of Political and Social Science* CXL (1928): 105–115.

———. "The New Community and its Future." *Annals of the American Academy of Political and Social Science* CXLIX (1930): 157–164.

Burgin, Miron. *The Economic Aspects of Argentine Federalism, 1820–1852.* Cambridge: Harvard University Press, 1946.

Canto, Estela. *El retrato y la imagen,* Buenos Aires: Editorial Losada, 1950.

de Caryevschi, Teresa Kaplanski, *Caracteristicas de los socios de la AMIA.* Buenos Aires: Institute de Investigaciones Sociales, 1970.

Chudacoff, Howard P. *Mobile Americans.* New York: Oxford University Press, 1972.

Ciria, Alberto. *Partidos y poder en la Argentina moderna (1930–1946).* Buenos Aires: Editorial Jorge Alvarez, 1968.

———, et al. *La década infame.* Buenos Aires: Carlos Perez Editor, 1969.

Cochran, Thomas C., et al. *Entrepreneurship in Argentine Culture.* Philadelphia: University of Pennsylvania Press, 1962.

Cohen, Martin A., ed. *The Jewish Experience in Latin American.* 2 vols. Waltham: American Jewish Historical Society, 1971.

Cohen, J. X. *Jewish Life in South America.* New York: Bloch Publishing Co., 1941.

Comité Judío Americano. *Comunidades judías de latinoamérica.* Buenos Aires: Comité Judio Americano, 1972.

Commons, John R., "The Sweating System in the Clothing Trade." In *Trade Unionism and Labor Problems,* pp. 316–335. Boston: Ginn and Co., 1905.

———. *Trade Unionism and Labor Problems.* Boston: Ginn and Co., 1905.

Cornblit, Oscar. "European Immigrants in Argentine Industry and Politics." In *The Politics of Conformity in Latin America,* edited by Caludio Véliz, pp. 221–248. New York: Oxford University Press, 1967.

———. *Immigrantes y empresarios en la politica argentina,* 2nd ed. Buenos Aires: Editorial del Instituto, 1967.

Corsi, Edward C. *Poland.* New York: Wyndham Press, 1933.

Cortes-Conde, Roberto, "Problemas del crecimiento industrial (1870–1914)." *Argentina: sociedad de masas,* edited by Torcuato Di Tella, et al. 1965, pp. 59–84.

Cuneo, Dardo, *Juan B. Justo.* Buenos Aires: Editorial Americalee, 1943.

Daireaux, Emilio. *Vida y costumbres en el plata.* 2 vols. Buenos Aires: Felix Lajouane, 1888.

Davis, Horace B. "Business Mortality: The Shoe Manufacturing Industry." *Harvard Business Review* XVII (Spring 1939): 331–338.

Dawidowicz, Lucy S., ed. *The Golden Tradition.* Boston: Beacon Press, 1967.

Delegación de Asociaciones Israelitas Argentinas (DAIA). *Cincuenta años de colonización judía en la Argentina.* Buenos Aires: DAIA, 1939.

Di Tella, Torcuato, et al., *Argentina: sociedad de masas.* Buenos Aires: Editorial Universitaria de Buenos Aires, 1965.

———, and Tulio Halperin-Donghi eds. *Los fragmentos del poder.* Buenos Aires: Editorial Jorge Alvarez, 1968.

Díaz Alejandro, Carlos F. *Essays on the Economic History of the Argentine Republic.* New Haven: Yale University Press, 1970.

Dickmann, Enrique. *Recuerdos de un militante socialista.* Buenos Aires: La Vanguardia, 1949.

Dubnow, S. M. *History of the Jews in Russia and Poland.* 3 vols. Philadelphia: Jewish Publication Society of America, 1916–1920.

El Diario Israelita. *Homenaje a "El Diario Israelita."* Buenos Aires: Comité de Homenaje a "El Diario Israelita," 1940.

Enciclopedia Judaica Castellana. vol. I–vol. II. Mexico: Editorial Enciclopedia Judaica Castellana, 1948.

Ernesto Tornquist y Cia., Ltd. *The Economic Development of the Argentine Republic in the Last Fifty Years*. Buenos Aires: Ernesto Tornquist y Cia., Ltd., 1919.

Errera, Leo. *The Russian Jews*. London: David Nutt, 1894.

Falcoff, Mark. "Raul Scalabrini Ortiz: The Making of an Argentine Nationalist." *Hispanic American Historical Review* LII (1972): 74–101.

Ferns, H. S. *Britain and Argentina in the Nineteenth Century*. Oxford: Clarendon Press, 1960.

Ferrer, Aldo. *The Argentine Economy*. trans. Marjorie Urquidi. Berkeley: University of California Press, 1967.

Fillol, Tomas R. *Social Factors in Economic Development*. Cambridge: MIT Press, 1961.

Fishman, William J. *Jewish Radicals*. New York: Pantheon Books, 1974.

Ford, A. G. *The Gold Standard, 1880–1914*. Oxford: Clarendon Press, 1962.

Frumkin, Jacob, et al. *Russian Jewry, 1860–1917*. New York: Thomas Yoseloff Ltd., 1966.

Gallo, Ezequiel and Silvia Sigal. "La formación de los partidos políticos contemporaneos: la UCR (1890–1916)," In *Argentina: sociedad de masas*, edited by Torcuato Di Tella, et al. 1965, pp. 124–176.

Garmendia, Dionisio Jorge. "Algunas consideraciones metodológicas sobre una investigacion de estratificación y movilidad sociales. *America Latina* IV (November 1968): 385–420.

Garrard, John. *The English and Immigration, 1880–1910*. London: Oxford University Press, 1971.

Gartner, Lloyd P. *The Jewish Immigrant in England, 1870–1914*. London: George Allen & Unwin, Ltd., 1960.

Gerassi, Marysa. *Los nacionalistas*. Buenos Aires: Editorial Jorge Alvarez, 1969.

Gerchunoff, Alberto. *Los gauchos judíos*. Buenos Aires: Editorial Universitaria de Buenos Aires, 1964.

Germani, Gino. *Estructura social de la Argentina*. Buenos Aires: Editorial Raigal, 1955.

———. "La sociología en Argentina." *Revista Latinoamericana de Sociología* IV (November 1968); 385–420.

———. "Movilidad social en la Argentina." In *Movilidad social en la sociedad industrial*, edited by S. M. Lipset and Reinhard Bendix, pp. 317–366. Buenos Aires: Editorial Universitaria de Buenos Aires, 1969.

———. "Mass Immigration and Modernization in Argentina." In *Masses in Latin America*, edited by Irving Louis Horowitz, pp. 289–330. New York: Oxford University Press, 1970.

———. "Mass Society, Social Class and the Emergence of Fascism." In *Masses in Latin America*. edited by Irving Louis Horowitz, pp. 577–600. New York: Oxford University Press, 1970.

————. *Politica y sociedad en una época de transición*. Buenos Aires: Editorial Paidos, 1971.

————. "Social Stratification and Its Historical Evolution in Argentina." *Rivista di studi sociali dell'Instituto Luigi Sturzo*, V (January 1971): 7–61.

Glicksman, William M. *In the Mirror of Literature*. New York: Living Books, 1966.

Godio, Julio. *La Semana Trágica de Enero 1919*. Buenos Aires: Grancia Editor, 1972.

Goodhart, Arthur L. *Poland and the Minority Races*. London: George Allen & Unwin, Ltd., 1920.

Goodwin, Paul B. "The Politics of Rate-Making: the British Owned Railways and the Unión Civica Radical." *Journal of Latin American Studies* VI (November 1974); 257–287.

Goren, Arthur A. *New York Jews and the Quest for Community*. New York: Columbia University Press, 1970.

Graciarena, Jorge and Maria A. R. Sautu. "La investigación de estratificación y movilidad social en el Gran Buenos Aires." America Latina IV (November 1961): 277–302.

Graham, Malbone W. "Polish Politics, 1981–1939." In *Poland,* edited by Bernadotte E. Schmitt, pp. 123–147. Berkeley: University of California Press, 1945.

Greenberg, Louis. *The Jews in Russia,* Vol. I and II. New Haven: Yale University Press, 1955.

Griffen, Clyde. "Occupational Mobility in Nineteenth Century America: Problems and Possibilities." *Journal of Social History*. (Spring, 1972): 310–330.

Halperin-Donghi, Tulio. *The Aftermath of Revolution in Latin America*. New York: Harper & Row, 1974.

Hauser, Philip M. and Leo F. Schnore eds., *The Study of Urbanization*. New York: John Wiley and Sons, 1967.

Hershberg, Theodore, et al., "Occupation and Ethnicity in Nineteenth Century Cities: A Collaborative Inquiry." *Historical Methods Newsletter* VII (June 1974): 174–216.

Hobson, John A. *The Evolution of Modern Capitalism*. London: George Allen & Unwin, Ltd., 1928.

Holdich, Sir Thomas H. *The Countries of the King's Award*. London: Hurst and Blackett, Ltd., 1904.

Horowitz, Irving Louis. "The Jewish Community of Buenos Aires." *International Review of Community Development* IX (1962):187–213.

————, ed. *Masses in Latin America*. New York: Oxford University Press, 1970.

Hoselitz, Bert F. *Sociological Aspects of Economic Growth*. New York: The Free Press, 1960.

Hourwich, Isaac A. *Immigration and Labor*. New York: B. W. Huebsch, Inc., 1922.

Howe, Irving. *World of Our Fathers*. New York: Harcourt, Brace, Jovanovich, 1976.

Hurvitz, S. *Colonia Lucienville*. Buenos Aires: 1932. In Yiddish.

Hutchinson, Bertram. "Social Mobility Rates in Buenos Aires, Montevideo, and Saõ Paulo: A Preliminary Comparison." *America Latina* (October–December 1962): 3–20.

————. "Urban Social Mobility Rates in Brazil Related to Migration and Changing Occupational Structure." *America Latina* VI (July–September 1963), 47–61.

Hutchinson, R. G., A. R. Hutchinson, and Mabel Newcomer. "A Study in Business Mortality." *American Economic Review* XXVIII (September 1938). 497–514.

Hyamson, A. M. *A History of the Jews in England*. London: Cleatto and Windus, 1908.

Imaz, José Luis de. *Los que mandan*. trans. Carlos Astiz. Albany: State University of New York Press, 1970.

Johnpoll, Bernard K. *The Politics of Futility*. Ithaca: Cornell University Press, 1967.

Josephs, Ray. *Argentine Diary*. New York: Random House, 1944.

Kallen, Horace M., *Frontiers of Hope*. New York: Horace Liveright, 1929.

Katz, Michael B. "Occupational Classification in History." *Journal of Interdisciplinary History* (Summer 1972): 63–88.

Kenworthy, Eldon. "The Function of the Little-Known Case in Theory Formation or What Peronism Wasn't." *Comparative Politics* VI (October 1973): 343–353.

Kligsberg, Bernardo. "La juventud judía en la Argentina." *Nueva Sion*. September 1971.

Knights, Peter. *The Plain People of Boston*. New York: Oxford University Press, 1971.

Koebel, W. H. *Argentina: Past and Present*. London: Adam and Charles Black, 1914.

Korn, Francis. *Buenos Aires: los huéspedes del '20*. Buenos Aires: Editorial Sudamerican, 1974.

LaBelle, Thomas J., ed. *Educational Alternatives in Latin America*. Los Angeles: UCLA Latin American Center Publications, 1975.

Lane, Frederic C. and Jellie C. Riemersma eds. *Enterprise and Secular Change*. Homewood: Richard D. Irwin, 1953.

Lee, Samuel J. *Moses of the New World*. New York: Thomas Yoseloff, 1970.

Leiserson, William. *Adjusting Immigrants and Industry*. New York: Harper and Brothers, 1924.

Lerner, Natan. "Anti-Semitism and the Nationalist Ideology in Argentina." *Dispersion and Unity:* 17–18, (1973).

Lestchinsky, Jacob. *Jewish Migration for the Past Hundred Years*. New York: YIVO, 1944.

———. "The Jews in the Cities of the Republic of Poland." *YIVO Annual of Jewish Social Science* I (1946): 156–177.

Levene, Ricardo. *A History of Argentina*. Trans. and ed. William Spence Robertson. Chapel Hill: University of North Carolina Press, 1937.

Levine, Louis. *The Women's Garment Workers*. New York: B. W. Huebsch, 1924.

Lewin, Boleslao. *El judío en la época colonial*. Buenos Aires: Colegio Libre de Estudios Superiores, 1939.

———. *Como fue la immigración judía a la Argentina*, Buenos Aires: Editorial Plus Ultra, 1971.

———. *La colectividad judía en la Argentina*, Buenos Aires: Alzamor Editores, 1974.

Liebermann, Jose. *Tierra Sonada*. Buenos Aires: Luis Lasserre y Cia., 1959.

———. *Los judíos en la Argentina*. Buenos Aires: Editorial Libra, 1966.

Light, Ivan H. *Ethnic Enterprise in America*. Berkeley: University of California Press, 1972.

Lipman, V. D. *Social History of the Jews in England, 1850–1950*. London: Routledge and Kegan Paul, 1954.

Lipset, Seymour Martin and Reinhard Bendix. *Movilidad social en la sociedad industrial*. Buenos Aires: Editorial Univeritaria de Buenos Aires, 1963.

———. "Research Problems in the Comparative Analysis of Mobility and Development." *International Social Science Journal* XVI (1964).

———. "Values, Education and Entrepreneurship." In *Elites in Latin America*, edited by Seymour Martin Lipset and Aldo Solari, pp. 3–60. New York: Oxford University Press, 1967.

———. *Elites in Latin America*. New York: Oxford University Press, 1967.

Lockwood, David, "The 'New' Working Class," *Archives Europeénes de Sociologie* I, (1960), 248–259.

Londres, Albert. *The Road to Buenos Aires*. New York: Horace Liveright, 1928.

López, Lucio V. *La gran aldea*. Buenos Aires: Editorial Claridad, n.d.

Luna, Félix. *Yrigoyen*. Buenos Aires: Editorial Raigal, 1954.

———, *Alvear*. Buenos Aires: Libros Argentinos, 1958.

Machray, Robert. *Poland, 1914–1931*. London: George Allen & Unwin, Ltd., 1932.

Mahler, Raphael. "Antisemitism in Poland." In Pinson, Koppel S. *Essays on Antisemitism*, edited by Koppel S. Pinson, pp. 111–144. New York. Conference on Jewish Relations, 1946.

Malach, Leon. "Two Generations in the Argentine." *The Menorah Journal* XIII (August 1927): 408–416.

Marcson, Simon, ed. *Automation, Alienation, and Anomie*. New York: Harper & Row, 1970.

Marotta, Sebastián. *El movimiento sindical argentina*. 3 vols. Buenos Aires: Editorial Lacio, 1960, 1961, 1970.

Martel, Julián (pseud.). La Bolsa. Buenos Aires: Biblioteca "La Nación," 1905.

Martínez, Albert B. and Maurice Lewandowski. *The Argentine in the Twentieth Century*. London: T. F. Unwin, 1911.

Mayer, Arno J. "The Lower Middle Class as Historical Problem." *Journal of Modern History* 47 (September 1975): 409–436.

Mendelsohn, Ezra. *Class Struggle in the Pale*. Cambridge: Cambridge University Press, 1970.

Mendelsohn, José. "Cincuenta años de vida judía en la Argentina." In *Cincuenta años de vida judía en la Argentina*. Edited by Hirsch Triwaks, pp. 63–66. Buenos Aires: Talleres Graficas Julio Kaufman. 1940.

Moore, Wilbert E. "Technological Change and the Worker." *Automation, Alienation, and Anomie,* edited by Simon Marcson, pp. 48–53. New York: Harper & Row, 1970.

Moreno, Juan Carlos. *Genio y figura de Hugo Wast*. Buenos Aires: Editorial Universiteria de Buenos Aires, 1969.

Morse, Richard M. "A Prolegomenon to Latin American Urban History." *Hispanic American Historical Review* LII (August 1972): 359–394.

Municipalidad de la Ciudad de Buenos Aires. *Evolución urbana de la ciudad de Buenos Aires*. Buenos Aires: Municipalidad de la Ciudad de Buenos Aires, 1972.

Nuñez, Luis F. *Los cementerios*. Buenos Aires: Ministerio de Cultura e Educaión, 1970.

Oddone, Jacinto. *Gremialismo proletario argentino*. Buenos Aires: La Vanguardia, 1949.

Ortiz, Ricardo M. *Historia económica de la Argentina, 1850–1930*. Buenos Aires: Editorial Plus Ultra, 1974.

Panettieri, José. *Los trabajadores*. Buenos Aires: Editorial Jorge Alvarez, 1968.

————. *Síntesis histórica del desarollo industrial argentino*. Buenos Aires: Editorial Macchi 1969.

Pareja, Ernesto M. *La prostitución en Buenos Aires*. Buenos Aires: TOR, n.d.

Park, Robert E. and Ernest W. Burgess. *The City*. Chicago: University of Chicago Press, 1925.

Patkin, A. L. *The Origins of the Russian-Jewish Labour Movement*. Melbourne: F. W. Chesire, Ltd., 1947.

Patroni, Adrián. *Los trabajadores en la Argentina*. Buenos Aires: n.p., 1897.

Phelps, Vernon L. *The International Economic Position of Argentina*. Philadelphia: University of Pennsylvania Press, 1938.

Pinson, Koppel S. "Arkady Kremer, Vladimir Medem, and the Ideology of the Jewish 'Bund.'" *Jewish Social Studies* VII (July 1945): 233–264.

Pinson, Koppel S., ed. *Essays on Antisemitism*. New York: Conference on Jewish Relations, 1946.

Pla, Alberto J. *Ideología y método en la historiografía argentina*, Buenos Aires: Ediciones Nueva Vision, 1972.

Potash, Robert A. *The Army & Politics in Argentina, 1928–1945*. Stanford: Stanford University Press, 1969.

Puiggros, Rodolf. *La democracia fraudulenta*. Buenos Aires: Editorial Jorge Alvarez, 1968.

Rapoport, Nicolás. "Breve historia del hospital." In *Libro del cincuentenario de la Ezrah y Hospital Israelita*, edited by Nicolas Rapoport, pp. 25–33. Buenos Aires: Talleres Gráficos Julio Kaufman, 1950.

Reiss, Albert J., ed. *Louis Wirth on Cities and Social Life*. Chicago: University of Chicago Press, 1964.

Rennie, Ysabel F. *The Argentine Republic*. New York: Macmillan Co., 1945.

Riasanovsky, Nicholas V. *A History of Russia*. New York: Oxford University Press, 1963.

Riis, Jacob. *How the Other Half Lives*. New York: Hill and Wang, 1957.

Rischin, Moses. *The Promised City*. New York: Harper & Row, 1962.

Rock, David. "Lucha civil en la Argentina: La Semana Trágica de Enero de 1919." *Desarollo Economico* 11 (July 1971–March 1972): 165–216.

———. "Machine Politics in Buenos Aires and the Radical party." *Journal of Latin American Studies* IV (November 1972): 233–256.

———. *Politics in Argentina, 1890–1930*. London: Cambridge University Press, 1975.

Rogger, Hans. "Tsarist Policy on Jewish Emigration," *Soviet Jewish Affairs* III (1973): 26–36.

Rojas, Ricardo. *La restauración nacionalista*. Buenos Aires, Ministerio de Justicia e Instrucción Publica, 1909.

Romero, José Luis. *El desarollo de las ideas en la sociedad argentina del siglo XX*. Mexico-Buenos Aires: Fondo de Cultura Economíca, 1965.

Rosenswaike, Ira, "The Jewish Population of Argentina." *Jewish Social Studies* XXII (October 1960): 195–214.

Roucek, Joseph S. "Minorities." In *Poland*. Edited by Bernadotte E. Schmitt, pp. 148–166. Berkeley: University of California Press, 1945.

Rubinstein, Juan Carlos, *Movilidad social en una sociedad dependiente*, Buenos Aires: Ediciones Corregidor, 1973.

Sargent, Charles. *The Spatial Evolution of Greater Buenos Aires*. Tempe: Arizona State University Press, 1974.

Sarmiento, Domingo F. *Conflicto y armonías de la razas en America*. Buenos Aires: La Cultura Argentina, 1915.

————. *Life in the Argentine Republic in the Days of the Tyrants*. New York: Collier Books, 1961.

Scheps, Abraham. *El aporte judío en le economia Argentina*, Buenos Aires: Primera Conferencia de Investigadores y Estudiosos, 1961.

Schmitt, Bernadotte E., ed. *Poland*. Berkeley: University of California Press, 1945.

————. "Rebirth of Poland, 1914–1923." In *Poland*. Edited by Bernadotte E. Schmitt, Berkeley: University of California Press, 1945.

Schnore, Leo F. "On the Spatial Structure of Cities in the Two Americas." In *The Sturdy of Urbanization*, edited by Philip M. Hauser and Leo F. Schnore, New York: John Wiley and Sons, 1967, pp. 347–398.

Schwartz, P. "Revolutionary Activities of the Jewish Labor Bund in the Czarist Army." *YIVO Annual of Jewish Social Science* XIII (1965): 227–242.

Scobie, James R. *Revolution on the Pampas*. Austin: University of Texas Press, 1964.

————. *Argentina: A City and A Nation*. 2nd ed. New York: Oxford University Press, 1970.

————. "Changing Urban Patterns: The Porteño Case, 1880–1910." *XXXVII International Congress of Americanists* 1: 323–338.

————. "Buenos Aires as a Commercial Bureaucratic City, 1880–1910." *American Historical Review* 77 (October 1972): 1034–1073.

————. *Buenos Aires: From Plaza to Suburb*. New York: Oxford University Press, 1974.

Sebreli, Juan Rosé, ed. *La cuestion judía en la Argentina*. Buenos Aires: Editorial Tiempo Contemporaneo, 1968.

————. *Buenos Aires: vida cotidiana y alienación*. Buenos Aires: Siglo Veinte, 1969.

Seidman, Joel. *The Needle Trades*. New York: Farrar and Rinehart, 1942.

Serta, Emilio. *Judíos de Buenos Aires; relatos de judíos*. Buenos Aires: Ediciones Feria, n.d.

Sharot, Stephen. "Religious Change in Native Orthodoxy in London, 1870–1914." *Jewish Journal of Sociology*, XV (June 1973): 57–78.

Shatzky, Jacob. *Communidades judías en latinoamérica*. Buenos Aires: Ediciones del American Jewish Committee, 1952.

Shpall, Leo, trans. "David Feinberg's Historical Survey of the Colonization of the Russian Jews in Argentina." *Publication of the American Jewish Historical Society*. XLIII (September 1953): 37–69.

Simmons, James W. "Changing Residence in the City: A Review of Intraurban Mobility." *Geographical Review*. 58 (October 1968): 622–651.

Singer, Isidore, ed. *Russia at the Bar of the American People*. New York: Funk and Wagnalls, 1904.

Smith, Peter H. *Politics & Beef in Argentina*. New York: Columbia University Press, 1969.

Snow, Peter. *Argentine Radicalism*. Iowa City: University of Iowa Press, 1965.

Sofer, Eugene F. "Argentine Jewry: What Do We Need to Know?" *Interchange* 1 (1977): 1–12.

Sofer, Eugene F. and Mark D. Szuchman, "Educating Immigrants: Voluntary Associations in the Acculturation Process." In *Educational Alternatives in Latin America,* edited by Thomas J. Labelle, pp. 334–359. Los Angeles: UCLA Latin American Center Publications, 1975.

Soiza Reilly. "El martirio de los inocentes," *Revista Popular,* vol. 2, n. 42 (February 3, 1919).

Solberg, Carl. *Immigration and Nationalism*. Austin: University of Texas Press, 1970.

———. "Tariff and Politics in Argentina, 1916–1930." *Hispanic American Historical Review*. LIII (May 1973): 260–284.

Solominsky, Nahum. *La Semana Trágica*. Buenos Aires: Biblioteca Popular Judia, 1971.

Solomonoff, Jorge N. *Ideologias del movimiento obrero y conflicto social*. Buenos Aires: Editorial Proyección, 1971.

Spalding, Hobart A., ed. *La clase trabajadora argentina*. Buenos Aires: Editorial Galerna, 1970.

Starr, Joshua. "Jewish Citizenship in Rumania, 1878–1940." *Jewish Social Studies*. III (January, 1941): 57–80.

Stephen, David. "The Radical Right in Latin America." *Wiener Library Bulletin*. XXII (Spring 1968): 25–30.

Stimson, Frederick J. *My United States*. New York: Charles Scribner's Sons, 1931.

Storni, Pablo. "La industria y la situación de las clases obreras en la Capital de la República." *Revista Juridica y de Ciencias Sociales*. XXV (October–December 1908): 237–321.

Swierenga, Robert P., ed. *Quantification in American History*. New York: Atheneum, 1970.

Szaikowski, Zosa. "Jewish Emigration Policy in the Period of the Rumanian 'Exodus' 1899–1903." *Jewish Social Studies*. XIII (January 1951): 47–70.

Szasz, Zsombor de. *The Minorities in Roumanian Transylvania*. London: Richards Press, 1927.

Szuchman, Mark D. and Eugene F. Sofer. "The State of Occupational Classification Studies in Argentina: A Classificatory Scheme." *Latin American Research Review*. XI (Spring 1976): 159–172.

Taeuber, Karl E. and Alma F. Taeuber. *Negroes in Cities*. New York: Atheneum, 1972.

Tcherikower, Elias, ed. *The Early Jewish Labor Movement in the United States*. trans. Aaron Antonovsky, New York: YIVO, 1961.

Thernstrom, Stephan. "The Dimensions of Occupational Mobility." In *Quantification in American History*. Edited by Robert P. Swierenga, pp. 366–388. New York: Atheneum, 1970.

————. *The Other Bostonians*. Cambridge: Harvard University Press, 1973.

Thompson, E.P. *The Making of the English Working Class*. New York: Vintage, 1966.

Tiempo, Cesar. *La campaña antisemita y el Director de la Biblioteca Nacional*. Buenos Aires: Ediciones DAIA, 1935.

Tobias, Henry J. *The Jewish Bund in Russia*. Stanford: Stanford University Press, 1972.

Tugan-Baranovsky, M.I. *The Russian Factory in the 19th Century*. trans. Arthur and Claora S. Levin. Homewood: Richard D. Irwin, 1970.

Turner, Thomas A. *Argentina and the Argentines*. London: S. Sonnenschein and Co., 1892.

Ugarteche, Félix de. *Las industrias del cuero en la República Argentina*, Buenos Aires: Talleres Graficos de Roberto Canals, 1927.

Vaisman, Sergio. "La 'Zwi Migdal,' una historia sepultada." *Redacción*, I (July 1973): 78–79.

Vazeilles, José. *Los socialistas*. Buenos Aires: Editorial Jorge Alvarez, 1967.

Véliz, Claudio, ed. *The Politics of Conformity in Latin America*. New York: Oxford University Press, 1967.

Verbitsky, Gregorio. *Rivera, afán de medio siglo*. Buenos Aires: Comision del cincuentenario de Rivera, 1955.

Vishniak, Mark. "Antisemitism in Tsarist Russia." In *Essays in Antisemitism*. Edited by Koppel S. Pinson, pp. 79–110. New York: Conference on Jewish Relations, 1946.

Von Laue, Theodore H. *Sergei Witte and the Industrialization of Russia*. New York: Atheneum, 1963.

Wald, Pinie. *The Jewish Working Class and Socialist Movement*. Buenos Aires: AMIA, 1963. In Yiddish.

Walter, Richard J. *The Socialist Party of Argentina, 1890–1930*. Austin: University of Texas Press, 1977.

Ward, David. "The Emergence of Central Immigrant Ghettoes in American Cities: 1840–1920." In *Internal Structure of the City*. Larry S. Bourne, ed. New York: Oxford University Press, 1971.

Webb, Beatrice. "The Diary of an Investigator." In *Problems of Modern Industry*, edited by Sidney and Beatrice Webb, pp. 1–19. London: Longman, Green, and Co., 1898.

————. "The Jews of East London." In *Problems of Modern Industry,* edited by Sidney and Beatrice Webb, pp. 20–45. London: Longman, Green, and Co., 1898.

Webb, Sidney and Beatrice Webb. *Problems of Modern Industry.* London: Longman, Green, and Co., 1898.

Weil, Felix. *The Argentine Riddle.* New York: John Day Co., 1944.

Weisbrot, Robert. "Antisemitism in Argentina." *Midstream.* XXIV (May 1978): 12–23.

————. "Jews in Argentina Today." *Judaism.* 25 (Fall 1976): 390–401.

Winsberg, Morton D. *Colonia Baron Hirsch.* Gainesville: University of Florida Press, 1963.

Wirth, Louis. *The Ghetto.* Chicago: University of Chicago Press, 1928.

————. "The Ghetto." In *Louis Wirth on Cities and Social Life,* edited by Albert J. Reiss, pp. 84–98. Chicago: University of Chicago Press, 1964.

Yans-McLaughlin, Virginia. "A Flexible Tradition: South Italian Immigrants Confront a New Work Experience." *Journal of Social History.* VII (Summer 1974): 429–445.

Yujovsky, Oscar. "Políticas de vivienda en la ciudad de Buenos Aires." *Desarollo Economico.* 14 (1974): 327–372.

Zarchin, Michael M. *Jews in the Province of Posen,* Philadelphia: Dropsie College, 1939.

Zaretz, Charles E. *The Amalgamated Clothing Workers of America,* New York: Ancon Publishers, 1934.

INDEX